CHILDREN'S
TOYS
THROUGHOUT THE AGES

LESLIE DAIKEN

Children's

throughout the ages

SPRING BOOKS · LONDON

To

ANTHONY AND CONSTANCE RYE

Originally published by B. T. Batsford Ltd

This edition first published 1963

Second impression 1965

© *Copyright Leslie Daiken*

Published by

SPRING BOOKS

Westbook House · Fulham Broadway · London

Printed in Czechoslovakia by Knihtisk, Prague

T 1437

LESLIE DAIKEN

Children's

throughout the ages

SPRING BOOKS · LONDON

To

ANTHONY AND CONSTANCE RYE

Originally published by B. T. Batsford Ltd

This edition first published 1963

Second impression 1965

© *Copyright Leslie Daiken*

Published by

SPRING BOOKS

Westbook House · Fulham Broadway · London

Printed in Czechoslovakia by Knihtisk, Prague

T 1437

CONTENTS

LIST OF ILLUSTRATIONS

Figure *Page*

ACKNOWLEDGMENTS

The Author and Publishers are indebted to the following for their valuable coopera-
tion, and for their kind permission to reproduce the illustrations in this book:

Bassett-Lowke Ltd. (Mr. M. H. Sell), 58—61, 63, 67; Beauchamp Bookshop
Ltd., 50, 112; Bethnal Green Museum (Mr. C. M. Wheatley), 2, 34, 50, 51, 67,
72, 86, 109; Britains Ltd. (Mr. Denis Britain), 37–49, 97–100; British Film
Institute, 5; Trustees of the British Museum, 3; Museum of Childhood, Edinburgh, 24; *Connaissance des Arts*, 9, 101, 104, 105; Educational Supply Association
Ltd., 7, 10; Mme F. Fastré, 114, 117; Mr. G. Goddard-Watts, 111; Miss Joyce
Holt, 95; Mr. N. E. C. Huddleston, 84; Miss Barbara Jones, 116; London Museum
(Messrs. M. R. Holmes and F. H. W. Sheppard), 55, 68, 102; Mr. A. Panting
(photographer), 6, 18, 33, 63, 64, 65, 66, 68, 71, 79, 82, 83, 117; Mr. A. Rye, 52,
64; The Trustees of the Toy Museum, 14, 16, 18–23, 29, 30, 33, 53, 54, 63, 64,
66, 70, 71, 76–79, 82, 87, 113, 118, 119; Mr. N. Tozer (photographer), 2, 57, 108;
Mrs. Alison Uttley, 93; The Director of the Victoria and Albert Museum, and
Mr. C. H. Gibbs-Smith, 4, 84, 108; Mr. A. E. Wilson, 106, 107.

For many helpful suggestions received, or for the use of material included in this
work, they wish to thank the following:

Paul and Marjorie Abbatt; Dr. A. Bettex, Zürich; Dr. C. Willett Cunnington.
Mr. L. E. Deval; Mr. F. J. Epps; Miss Lesley Gordon; Mr. L. F. Hill; Mrs.
Madeleine Holloway; Mr. F. Mayer; Mr. G. Morice; Mr. E. C. Morel; Miss
Marjorie Parkes; Mr. L. G. G. Ramsey; Mr. F. L. Rees; Mr. F. Riley; Mr. E. F.
Saunders; Mr. D. Snelgrove; Dr. James Starkey, Dublin; Mr. F. R. B. White-
house, M. B. E.; and Dr. S. Yale.

They must also thank the following Authors and Publishers for granting permission
to quote from the books and magazine articles listed:

Apollo Magazine Ltd., English Silver Toys by Charles Oman; Architectural
Press Ltd., *Unsophisticated Arts* by Barbara Jones; C. W. Beaumont, *Flashback,
Stories of My Youth*; Country Life Ltd., The Westbrook Baby House by G.
Bernard Hughes; Gordon Graig, *Book of Penny Toys;* Geographical Magazine,
London, Geography in the Victorian Nursery by Percy Muir; Hodder and
Stoughton Ltd., *Trumpeter, Sound!* by D. L. Murray; John, Prince of Löwen-
stein, *Proclaim Freedom;* and the Executors of the late H. G. Wells, *Floor
Games*.

The tailpieces on pages 20, 28, 101, 171 and 181 are from wood engravings by
Thomas Bewick.

I

INTRODUCTION

Toys, like childhood itself, mean different things to different people. The bone-bare definitions as found in cautious dictionaries may have a point of concurrence; but the associations of the word, in different languages, vary according to the culture which produced that word. It is, indeed, remarkable how, as so often occurs in the spoken language, a term becomes part of current usage, and although it communicates a common idea to all who use it, in its associative usage it remains essentially personal.

To the parent, a toy is something to keep the child amused; abstracted always, instructed sometimes. If the adult intends to demonstrate an action, or participate in any pattern of play, he then will want to share in the pleasures of playing, salvaging his own childhood from under the crust of his later experience.

Adult playing is still appreciably what it was when Neolithic man fingered a chip of bone in his darkened cave; when Hero invented the first water-bubbling bird-whistle, a century and a half before the Christian era; or even earlier, as was the manner of the oriental kings who in their magnificence employed artificers and smiths to fashion golden nightingales, with gilt enamelling, and set them

> "upon a golden bough to sing
> To lords and ladies of Byzantium"

—an image which haunted the poet Yeats as he approached the winter of his life. And so, we still deceive ourselves into believing, that it is entirely for children that we provide playthings, whereas it is we ourselves, as often as not, who feel an irresistible urge to play with them.

The layman is not alone in his subjective notions of what constitutes a toy. Even among specialists, when we come to consider a toy in relation to function, quality or value, wide differences of connotation exist.

How rich in the nomenclature of diversion and sport is the English language! So well-endowed is it, compared with others, that the Oxford Dictionary, under *toy*, lists no less than six sub-sections. The associative meanings embraced by this powerful, evocative and apocalyptic word, relate to entertainment—in such terms as *fun, amusement* and *sport;* to human caprice in such terms as *antic, trick, jest, joke* and *conceit;* to human folly in such as *trifle, nonsense, trumpery* or *rubbish.* The animate is indicated in *pet* (for a lapdog, presumably) and the inanimate article in a range of ideas conveyed by such terms as *model, trinket, gewgaw, knick-knack.* As though these were not sufficient to communicate shades of meaning, we have as an alternative to the Old English specific *teon,* which means *to draw* or *to lead* (origin of the pull-toy), the generic concept of *plaything,* the article which, together with the player, completes the game-pattern. And this derives also from a Germanic root, *i.e. pleg(i)an*—to play.

To the psychologist, *toys* are a means of measuring the extent of a child's "engram-complexes," or analysing its behaviour. To the Froebel teacher in a modern kindergarten, *toys* represent Play Material, used consciously to augment the syllabus, and with a deliberate pedagogic aim. To the designer, *toys* present an exercise in producing something which will be constructionally sound, easy to make, pleasant to feel and to look at, and economical in price. In these considerations he is governed both by the manufacturer and the customer.

The philosopher sees, reflected in the careful selection of playthings, a ladder to a child's moral and social self, just as of old the Hellenic ideals of life and conduct were fostered by the great games. The anthropologists' views divide on their interpretations. One theory, following the studies of Karl Groos,[1] regards playing with toys, biologically considered, as anticipatory, *i.e.* analogous to the actions of animals which rehearse the battles of life, and acquire the necessary muscular equipment, in the way that a kitten rolls a ball of wool as he will, later, hunt a mouse. Another school holds the view that the patterns of play are reminiscent, *i.e.* a response to the reawakening of racial memories, which have in some way or another a direct value for juvenile development in every epoch. Such hypotheses, as advanced by Stanley Hall,[2] are strengthened by the contributions of educators, notably Sir Percy Nunn,[3] who has extended the theory to take in what he calls the hormic and the mnemic, a combination of the elements remembered from the race's history, and the sublimation through play of men's innate creative expression.

There is, furthermore, a trend in opinion which regards all forms of

[1] Karl Groos, *The Play of Animals.*
[2] Stanley Hall, *Adolescence,* Vol. I, chap. III.
[3] Sir Percy Nunn, *Education, Its Data and First Principles.*

play as the discharge of superfluous energy. This, on the other hand, has been countered by writers who argue that working with toys is essentially recreative; that instead of releasing pent-up energy, the process places new energy at the disposal of the organism, in the way that a tired child forgets the monotony of his tasks through the digression of a game; or an adult will return to exhausting work refreshed from a game of billiards or golf.[1]

These attitudes towards play and playthings multiply as we begin to look through the catalogue of interests. Thus the interest of an artist and illustrator is to portray the animation in a toy, its personality, its sense either of warmth or remoteness. The photographer, on the contrary, focusing his eye on the form and texture of the thing, is concerned not so much with its *quiditas*, its psyche, as the realistic image of its physical existence in time, which through his camera study he attempts to give us. It is, perhaps, for this reason that photographs of prehistoric finds in museum collections always seem to be devoid of reality: since being isolated and removed from such natural contexts as brick, glass, tiling or wood they are seldom shown related pictorially to the culture which produced them.

Similarly, the feeling for toys will differ according to whether the speaker is a teacher or a therapist; an archaeologist or an historian; a folk-lorist or a poet.

The poet's more universal comprehension, when compressed in the heroic couplets of which Pope is a master, presents facets of human experience philosophically, and interprets a wealth of observation with consummate skill in these well-known lines:

> "Behold the child, by Nature's kindly law
> Pleased with a rattle, tickled with a straw:
> Some livelier plaything gives his youth delight,
> A little louder but as empty quite:
> Scarfs, garters, gold amuse his riper stage,
> And beads and prayer-book are the toys of age.
> Pleased with this bauble still, as that before,
> Till tired he sleeps, and life's poor play is o'er." [2]

But howsoever to different types of men, and at different stages of their manhood, the art of play makes diverse claims, to the child, fortunately, the word *toy* always means the same thing. For children, toys have only one use; a purpose which is world-wide, ritualistic

---

[1] Sir Percy Nunn, *Education, Its Data and First Principles.*

[2] Pope, *Essay on Man.*

and supra-national; something common to all present-day cultures; having the same implication in all vocabularies. A toy, simply, is something to have fun with. And it is to consecrate this Spirit of Fun, *induced through a plaything*, that this book was first conceived.

Scholars more learned, and toy historians more qualified than I, have devoted long years to the study of this subject. They have left us books and monographs, notebooks and essays[1] which are fine contributions to human knowledge. To such writings and revelation we feel supremely indebted, for it is on the solid researches by investigators from the Old World that so much valuable superstructure has been erected by historians in the New World. To the delvings and dreamings, the reminiscences and speculations of Europeans— whether the Frenchman Henri René d'Allemagne[2] at the turn of the century; the German writer Karl Gröber[3] whose fine illustrated book appeared in the 'twenties; the English scholar Mrs. Nevill Jackson; who first chronicled data from many lands; or the Czech artist E. Herčík,[5] who, more recently, produced in colour his studies of folk-toys from Central Europe and the Slav peoples—it is by means of these links with the genesis of Western civilisation that a chain of scholarship has encompassed many peoples and lands.

It is this very universality in play which Professor Huizinga discovered in his work *Homo Ludens*. Having examined all the significant theories, he argues that it would be "perfectly possible to accept nearly all the explanations without coming much nearer to a real understanding of the play-concept. . . ." He goes on to disapprove of the quantitative methods of experimental science which "attack play directly, without paying attention to its profoundly aesthetic quality."

Nothing has since been said to refute this statement or weaken its implications. His conclusion is that the "intensity of, and absorption in, play finds no explanation in biological analysis. Yet in this intensity, this absorption, this power of maddening, lies the very essence, the primordial quality of play.";

Those of us who reflect on our childish preoccupation with certain toys, while others failed to interest us, will admit that it is in this

---

[1] Bibliography, pp. 197—201.
[2] H. R. d'Allemagne, *Histoire des Jouets*.
[3] Karl Gröber, *Children's Toys of Bygone Days*.
[4] *Toys of Other Days*.
[5] Herčík, Prague, 1951.
[6] Huizinga, 1949.

2. Dancing figure of British "Tommy" carved by a prisoner of war, *c*. 1916.

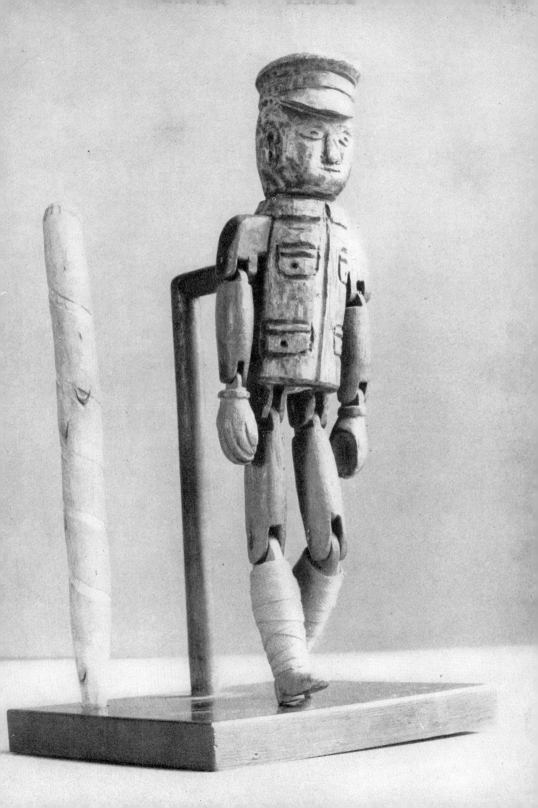

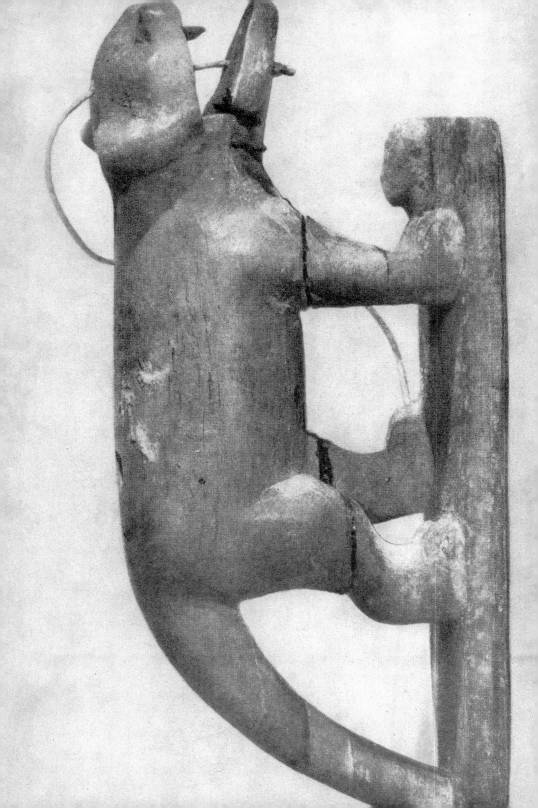

fierce concentration of childhood that our tastes and our prejudices, even our aptitudes, were formed; that these are projected-up right through adult life, in peculiar and typical patterns. It seems certain that many of us could reasonably trace the germ of an adult recreative hobby, a vocational spark or an occupational aptitude to day when we were impressed deeply by the structure of potentiality of some special plaything which commanded our whole being with an unearthly attraction.

Occasionally in our history toys have been desecrated by an adult consciousness which unleashed the elements of cruelty or the forces of sadism. One thinks of the comic figures devised in Nuremburg, with spaces cut out to hold the struggling head of an entrapped live bird, which by its panic gave all kinds of grotesque movements to these figures. The eighteenth-century catalogue describing these contrivances boasted that "no one would imagine that a living bird was inside, but would suppose that it was clockwork which made the head, eyes and beak of the bird move."

Such devilish ingenuity merely carried one stage further the device of the Italian mathematician, one Junellus Turrianus, who, to delight the Emperor Charles V, used to send up wooden sparrows into the King's chamber, "which did fly about there and returned with such marvellous artifice that the Superior of the Order of St. Jerome, being unskilled in the Mathematicks, suspended it for witchcraft."[1]

One remembers, in times more recent, more dark and more evil than those were, the miniature whips, knouts and instruments of torture that the Nazis put into the hands of children, instructing them in the accurate use of such gewgaws as a rehearsal for the fuller life.

Yet if we call such depravity shocking, is this really so far removed from the model guillotines[2] which a great French genius, during the Revolution, gave to little patriots for the beheading of toy aristocrats?

What strikes one most forcibly in the story of man's inhumanity to man is, that during wars and murder-matches, when "kill-or-be-killed" is the burthen issuing from the musical-box-cum-bandwagon, the most desperate of slaughterers suddenly become dreamers.

War-weary men, trained for carnage, suddenly become hungry for hearth and home; and, thinking of its warmth and the peace which they had known there, they turn to making—toys! Those prisoners

[1] Wm. Turner, *A Compleat History,* 1697 (Knick-knacks and Curiosities).
[2] Goethe's *Letter to His Son.*

String-operated toy: tiger with movable jaw, Egyptian, *c.* 1100 B.C.

of the Napoleonic Wars held at Norman Cross in Huntingdonshire differed so little in this respect from the Germans and Italians who were compounded in prisoner-of-war camps dotted over these islands during the prosecution of World War II.

Moreover, no social surveys were taken, nor were any records kept, of the hundreds of figurines, gadgets and models, crudely carved out of wood or knocked together by the "bloke wot has the file," somewhere in Flanders or in the *Stalags* during the 1914-1918 conflict. Nobody has chronicled the chapter whose hero is some grotesque-faced dancing doll, and its supporting rod, a piece of folk-art into which some Tommy carved endless days of heartache, and which today lies forgotten in a museum showcase, incongruous, a grimacing memorial to a love of toys and play that makes the whole world kin (2).

Indeed, it is one of the mysteries of our society that children the whole world over dramatise their love and other tender emotions by the agency of the very same playthings, just as they enact the same singing games to the same themes.[1]

[1] Robert Jarman, *Sangspiel;* and Curwen's edition *Folk-dances of Europe.*

II

TOYS THAT TEACH

THE giving of instruction and pleasure through play was a commonplace in the nursery long before the phrase "Educational Toys" was coined. Pedagogical advance in the twentieth century has achieved much, particularly in the fields of Child Development and modern Nursery Psychology, where great strides have been made to correlate play as a function of childhood with play as a function of the kindergarten and junior school.[1]

There is no doubt that educational development in England owes much to the great pioneers who hailed from the Continent. Such names as those of Montessori and Froebel are as lighthouses casting their beams over hitherto uncharted waters.

From Vienna especially, as from the Scandinavian countries also, Britain has been stimulated in evolving its own nursery methodology. These influences have led, likewise, to a more consciously educational design for toys,[2] of which the effect for good is now being widely felt.

Whereas Nursery Education owes much to those campaigners and theorists who have perfected Method, the artists, craftsmen, designers and producers of play materials and equipment are often inclined to be overlooked.[3]

Long before Educational Playthings were put on the market, toys had their intrinsic educational value. The earliest marble, the crudest wooden animal with moving jaws, the bouncing ball or the spinning top—were these not intrinsically educational? Is not pinning the tail on the donkey educational; knocking down the skittles, or dressing the doll? If we were to be logical, we should argue that the first "educational" toy is the baby-rattle. Percy H. Muir, writing on *Geography in the Victorian Nursery*, observed that Victorian ways with children were not as ours. Education was largely then a question of cramming.

[1] Beatrix Tudor Hart, *Play and Toys in Nursery Years*.
[2] Records of the Educational Supply Association.
[3] Margaret Costa, *Uncommon Pleasures*, p. 43 (Contact Books No. 17).

"The minds of children," he pointed out, "were regarded as jam pots, and the object of education as the cramming into them of as much jam as the receptacles could be persuaded to contain . . . pompous verbiage [showed] not only the didactic nature of the toys but a general air of regarding children as miniature grown-ups . . ."[1]

It was on a path winding from Mr. Muir's painstaking research into the mid-nineteenth-century toyland that my footsteps were led to the 1851 exhibits at the Victoria and Albert Museum. There, the catalogue quotes Faraday as having said that "boys' toys are the most philosophical things in the world," to which Mr. Muir adds that the toys of the "gentler sex" are more concerned with the kinder feelings of the heart: tenderness, love and the domestic virtues. During the 1851 Exhibition, in the room normally devoted to Parlour Games, were displayed some delightful and original Victorian "educational" inventions; such, for example, as the Zoëtrope, a mechanical toy open at the top, with a series of slits in the circumference and a number of figures representing successive positions of a moving object arranged around the inner surface (5). These, when viewed through the slits while the cylinder is in rapid rotation, produce the impression of the actual movement of the object.

Another toy illustrates the persistence of visual impression. This consists of a card or disc with figures drawn on the two sides which are apparently combined into one when the disc is rotated rapidly.

Nobody would challenge the contention, for example, that polyramas, cut-outs, jigsaws, teetotums and illustrated playing-cards are every bit as "educational" as the scores of board games constantly being put out by London merchants, or those puzzles which never grow out-moded. *Changeable Portraits of Ladies* (1819) is a series of pictures in which each head is separated into three movable parts and the changing of any one of these parts produces a new face (11). The instructions state that "21,952 different portraits can be made from the contents of the box"!

Building bricks, now known as Constructional Toys, letter and number cards, together with other material to encourage spelling, writing, drawing or telling the time, were in widespread use a hundred years ago (8). It is rewarding to compare the basic elements in their design, and to observe how little they have changed down the years.

While Victorian didacticism was concerned with diagnosing "the useful" for educational purposes, it nevertheless looked more and

[1] *The Geographical Magazine,* November 1946.

4. Early juvenile magic lantern, *c.* 1880
5. The Zoëtrope or "Wheel of Life", with animated strips, *c.* 1870

6. Hand-operated game of changing pictures, *c.* 1850
7. Contemporary jigsaw numbers designed by Peter Parkinson for E.S.A.

more to scientific invention to demonstrate to children the wonders of the laboratory.

Unusual stress was placed upon the science of optics, which, from 1880 onwards added each year a new apparatus to a growing list of exciting inventions. The vogue had begun with the developments in photography and the technical improvements which these had brought to the Magic Lantern (4). The latter had been first thought of by Roger Bacon in the thirteenth century, but in its newest form is ascribed to an Italian, Kircher, whose description of it appeared in 1650 in Rome, entitled *Ars Magnum et Umbrae.*

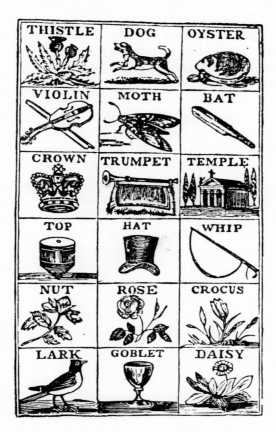

8. A late-eighteenth-century card for teaching spelling. *From Edwin Pearson's "Banbury Chap Books,"* 1890

By 1840 lanterns, slides and lenses were being produced in England, France and America for educational purposes. Old catalogues describe these as having been made of bronzed tin and very ornamental. They had Focus Tube, with cap to cover when not in use and keep from breaking. "Lamp, Reflector and twelve assorted long, slipping slides of Comic, Nursery and Fairy Tales etc. Each Lantern packed in a wooden box, is complete with directions printed in English, ready for use." Prices were from about seven shillings and sixpence.

The Germans concentrated on lens-making, and so were able to capture the growing demand for Magic Lanterns. In America one inventor turned out a cheap type called "The Polyopticon." "At the money, nothing will furnish a more varied and attractive source of entertainment," cajoled his advertisement.

A French gadget called the Panoptique was the forerunner of an opaque projector, or Magascope. This substitued for the customary glass slides home-made pictures cut out of books or periodicals which were projected on a screen. Many of these slides, or card sets, were inspired by high moral principles, with suitable captions. Then scriptural subjects were introduced; later, pictures from such writers as Bunyan. As an interest extended into the profane and the secular, such subjects as geography, "miracles of science," and nature study were added to the magic lantern's repertoire.

At that time the words *scope* and *scopic* were almost household words. As soon as a scientific discovery was launched, replicas adapted for the nursery were quickly manufactured. Brewster's experiments with optical instruments had led to the kaleidoscope. It was not long before this had been released as a child's toy. Fragments of coloured glass were put into a tube fitted at the end with three mirrors so placed as to form a hollow triangle. By rotating the tube, and, with one eye looking through the telescope-like instrument, the child could obtain an infinite number of changing symmetrical patterns.

Mention has also been made of the Zoëtrope (5), a toy utilising optical illusory movement, which was the newest thing around the eighteen-fifties. Other "scopic" entertainments of the late nineteenth century were afforded by such toys as the Phenakistescope and the Thaumatrope, both of which enjoyed brief spells of fashion.

A simpler version of illusory movement toys was invented in 1876 by a French scientist, Bellair. He called it a Chromotrope, and it involved the use of torsion applied to coloured discs. By threading string through a central hole in the discs, and exploiting its tensile strength in a pulling and relaxing action, colourful optical effects were produced. About thirty years later this idea took a different form when the cartoon booklet became a source of entertainment, especially to pupils, who improvised their own drawings on the corners of copybooks or school texts. Every page showed the same figure or groups of figures in a slightly different pose. By flicking the pages quickly, an effect of animated movement was obtained.

It should be remembered that all this preoccupation with optics, animated movement and stereoscopic vision were manifestations on the juvenile level of the tremendous advance being made by the science of photography and its allied branches. In one sense that mounting wave of successive devices was an anticipatory expression of an ungratified need for moving-pictures. In the same way Turrianus' experiments with flying birds indicated the yearning of the Renaissance mechanicians to create a machine that would emulate flight and conquer the air.

When the motion-picture was eventually perfected, and the toys of optical movement had reached their apex in miniature projectors and sixteen-millimetre comic films on celluloid strip, it is odd how the fashionable box-stereoscope, designed for children, went out of favour. Not till half a century afterwards, when stereoscopic vision has become a reality in the motion-picture field, do we find a return to pocket viewers (made compactly of black plastic),[1] and reflect on how scientific trends in the adult's world are quickly translated into children's toys giving those trends educational point.

The use of magnetised steel to induce movement returned in 1952 as a novel way of providing amusement. The donkey with the magnetised jaw who will turn towards a similarly treated carrot; the cat whose flexible paw will pounce on a magnetised mouse; the small insect that is attracted to some toy victim's nose—these are all revivals of toys which followed from laboratory experiments made at Dublin University as early as 1838.[2]

The educational value of experimental chemistry led the Victorian father to encourage his boys to work with chemicals. Much of this energy may have been dissipated in minor explosions. The making, for instance, of fireworks gave children a sound understanding of chemical action and reaction. Similarly, they learned from these forms

[1] *Games and Toys Year-Book for 1952*, p. 89.
[2] Records of the School of Physics, Trinity College, Dublin.

of investigation how chemistry adapted gas in rubber balloons; why a filled balloon is lighter than air; the principles upon which the catherine-wheel rotates, the rocket ascends, the magnet attracts, the steam-engine generates, and the electric supply transmits power.

Such forms of instruction, advocated by writers like Erle, who were ahead of their times, have entirely justified themselves. They were fundamentally sound and in contra-distinction to such Victorian notions as segregating toys into those suitable for boys only, and those for girls only.

Playing with toys according to such regulations, never together but always in groups of the same sex, has been abandoned by modern co-educational practice. In nursery schools and day nurseries where dolls' houses are part of the play equipment, it has been observed that there is no *natural* tendency for children of the under-six groups to split into divided camps. The normal boys want to share in the play with the girls, and together look after the dolls and arrange the furniture. By the same token, the girls welcome the opportunity of sharing in the play with trains and soldiers, which our grandparents believed were reserved for boys only, just as the proper place for little girls was beside a doll's house.

Whatever may be argued for and against Victorian ideas of using toys for strictly instructional ends, much of their trials and errors have been appreciated by those who specialise in the designing of play material for modern educational needs. Nowadays, the majority of leading toy-designers work closely with the teachers and pedagogues rather than with the managers of the workshops executing the orders. In this way the specifications come directly from the teachers and are, invariably, the result of careful observation in the playrooms and practical experience in the classrooms—the places where pediarchic play[1] registers any benefits it may confer upon the child.

[1] W. Watson, *Scottish Children's Games* (a paper read to the Folk Lore Society).

9. French table game, eighteenth century

10. Contemporary table games, designed by Peter Parkinson for E.S.A.

11. *Changeable Portraits of Ladies, c.* 1819
12. Set of hand-coloured cards of eighteenth-century characters

III

TOYS THAT MOVE—I

EACH historian has his own formula for classifying toys. Divisions and sub-divisions are evolved according to his aim or purpose. Yet in considering our subject there are two main factors which seem to divide toys naturally into two basic categories. Broadly speaking, *toys that move* and *toys that do not move* offer a satisfying classification.

Though *stasis* in a toy may give delight and claim attention every whit as much as the state of mobility, though it may provoke wonder or stimulate fancy, it is nevertheless *the principle of movement* that runs through the history and development of toys, like a single cord binding together a diversity of strands.

It is through movement that the educational value in playing with toys is effectually induced. This has been touched upon in the previous chapter. Whereas educationalists are agreed upon the essentials of manipulation and physical handling, it is *by movement* that children, and grown-ups likewise, first become aware of ordinary scientific principles.

Spin a top—and by this act discover, more finally than either written instruction or laboratory theory, the implications of dynamic movement or inertia. What better than the simple humming-top to demonstrate the Archimedean method of propulsion ?[1]

Roll a marble; bounce a ball; hit a skittle; turn a handle; or pull a cord. Each of these actions, in its own way, teaches the child something about how things move, in a manner freed from the obvious intent to teach; hence the value of instructional play.

Whether it is by the simple action of striking a mascot dangling over its head in its crib or its perambulator, whether it is through playing with a silver bell or a bone-handled rattle, the growing infant is subconsciously finding out a great deal about things, in addition to developing merely a tactile sense.

No more rewarding study confronts the educationalist than this genesis of movement, and its development in the toy, through examples both manually induced and automatic.

[1] T. W. Erle, *Science in the Nursery.*

13. Early Victorian toys, illustrating the principles of movement. *From T. W. Erle's "Science in the Nursery,"* 1884

To demonstrate general subjects within the school curriculum, *i.e.* history, handicrafts, dancing, music or science, through the visual aid of toys from many lands, with their great range and variety of movements, seems to be the ideal teaching approach of our times. Teachers would soon derive from working models and traditional games a vivid and compelling kind of material on which their lessons could be based: material with a potentiality for stimulating interest and perpetuating enthusiasm, more worthwhile perhaps than some of the Visual Aids which modern practice has casually accepted.

Particularly applicable for this purpose of bringing toys before the large bodies of spectators is the television screen; and this has inevitably take its place in the modern school as a teaching aid.[1] Through the television vehicle, toys of unique historical, artistic or scientific value could be shown to thousands of pupils at the same time. Each teacher can focus attention on those aspects of a subject which demonstrate the important points in a particular lesson.[2]

From the graphic records of ancient Egypt, from the evidence of Greek and Roman writings, we know that the ball game was elaborated as a game of skill for young and old. Throw-balls made from wood and composition, from papyrus and plaited reeds and cane are among the Egyptian exhibits at the British Museum.[3] Peoples still in a primitive stage of society weave these toys from grasses or coiled straw. Deer-hide is the material used by Red Indian tribes.

The very first ball to bounce was probably made from the inflated bladder of a sheep or goat, and early football games enjoyed by the Celts, and subsequently by the Anglo-Normans who learned the tradition from them, were contested with the bladder-type.[4] Wooden balls, such as used in bowls or skittles, were first crude affairs which became smooth with use and time, but in the seventeenth century highly polished hardwoods were used; later, ebony. The Japanese made throw-balls from soft tissue paper pressed tightly and bound with fancy string.[5] Paper was the earliest filling used for nursery play-balls, and in turn rags, sawdust, kapok and shavings and soft materials were tried.

[1] Naomi Capon, *The Child and the Dragon* (*B.B.C. Quarterly*, Vol. VI, No. 1).
[2] L. Daiken, *Teaching Through Play*, Pitman.
[3] Gwen White, *A Book of Toys*, pp. 6, 7.
[4] L. Daiken, *Children's Games Throughout the Year*.
[5] B. H. Chamberlain, *Things Japanese*, 1880; Best, *Games and Pastimes of the Maori*, Pt. V.

The utilisation of rubber, about a century ago, in the manufacture of bouncing balls completely revolutionised their design. It also multiplied their numbers and caused the rubber ball to be known in places hitherto unfamiliar to it. The elastic kernel contained by the golf ball, the solid black rubber from which the handball is made, the hollow cloth-coated tennis ball, or the spongy rubber substance and fleece-covered balloons given for safety to toddlers—these are, today, so universally taken for granted that we are apt to forget that not so long ago solid glazed pottery, heavy alabaster and rubbed marble were once bowled along a carpeted floor or a rolled lawn—ancestors on a grander scale of the diminutive marble.

Marbles came to medieval England from the Low Countries. Some of the early ones, known as bosses or bonces, and sometimes as King Marbles, were of stone or clay. They measured about four inches in diameter. The most highly prized were made of agate; the most common of baked clay, glazed and burnt in furnaces.[1] As a popular toy they reached their zenith towards the 1860's and 1870's in this country. The most highly prized were the veined glass Victorian marbles, are now very rare and are already regarded as collectors' pieces. These have been described sympathetically as glass spheres holding "a twisted spiral of filaments, thin music translated into coloured glass, crimson with pale blue, fire with canary, emerald with rose. The similar sphere of the eye, however, closely juxtaposed to the harder crystal, peers in vain through the twined colours to see a heart."[2]

A toy, now extinct, but which saw its heyday in Victorian England, is bilboquet, or cup and ball (15). It came to this country from France. The specimen preserved in the Victoria and Albert Museum is of lacquered wood and patterned with a motif of Italianate elegance. It measures about twelve inches long. Examples in the Muir Collection range from miniatures in ivory, about three inches long, with the ball about the size of a pea, to others about five or six inches long, made from tortoiseshell. The method of playing with this toy is described as follows in a handbook on fashionable games current in 1859:

"A ball of ivory or hard wood is attached to a stem of the same substance, having a shallow cup at one end, and a point at the other. The player holds the stem in his right hand, as shown in the figure, and having caused the ball to revolve, by twirling it in between the finger and thumb of his left hand, he jerks it up, and catches it, either in the cup or upon the spike, to receive which a hole is made in the ball. We need scarcely say that latter feat can only be performed by a skilful player."

[1] L. Daiken, *Children's Games Throughout the Year*, p. 171.
[2] Barbara Jones, *The Unsophisticated Arts*.

14. After the musical automaton and before the phonograph came this Polypho*
c. 1880, with metal discs

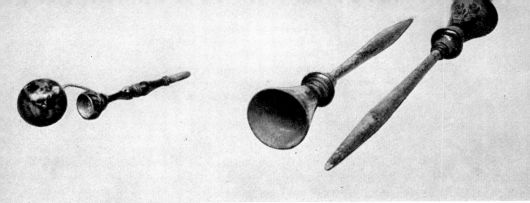

15. Cup and ball, and a pair of bilboquet cups, *c.* 1820

16. Chinese snake of jointed bamboo; realistic movement is induced by holding
the tail horizontally

17. Dutch educational game; coloured blocks depict the Arts and foreign lands,
c. 1780

Cup and ball was the favourite pastime of the Court of Henry III of France.

Some historians are convinced that the top first developed, as a conscious form of amusement, in Japan. Indeed, in Japan's national life top-play enjoys a status similar to kite-play in China. In China spinning-tops are traditionally made from conch shells which are levelled down at the head and weighted with lead at the tip. The conventional way of starting the spinning action in Eastern countries is by means of a string, and it seems likely that, as occurred with the kite, the string-propelled top was brought to Europe by Dutch seamen who had seen them used by natives in foreign parts.

By the middle of the sixteenth century the whip-top had become an adult toy in England. Old engravings[1] depict large models which where put at the disposal of peasants for their diversion by a local patron or by order of the ruling sovereign.

In contrast to the East, where hundreds of different kinds of tops are known, about six types are popular in England: the Spanish, or peg-top; the whip-top; the hand-twirled top of bone with its long spindle at the head, which could be propelled skilfully on the polished table surface. Or these, some finely wrought examples are to be found in the Bussell Collection now in the possession of Mr. Percy Muir. Then there is the pinching-top, where a spring wound about the top-spindle is released by a pinching action of the top head. A unique example of the latter is in the Holt Collection. It is of varnished wood and has the Union Jack painted on it, under some slogan supporting the Boer War. The string-driven humming-top was a coveted indoor toy in the Victorian nursery and a special souvenir model was produced for the 1851 Exhibition, with the Crystal Palace depicted on it.

Through the spinning motion of the top we apprehend a great deal more than just the whirring sound, the simple buzz, the erratic leap or the drunken collapse. European whip-tops and peg-tops could have derived from Chinese games. Yet on examining all the evidence one still remains unsatisfied that in its origin the simple spinning-top did not evolve from the spindle-whorl as used in simple forms of spinning. A scrutiny of examples of tops made by the natives of the Islands of Torres Straits tends to support this theory.

On the other hand, there is much to be said for the contention that they developed from wooden fire-drills. Against this, however, is the

[1] *Douce Folios,* Bodleian Library, Oxford.

fact that, with few exceptions, these fire-drills are without any form of fly-wheel at all, and are nearly always actuated by rubbing between the palms of the hands, or, in the instance of the Eskimo, by means of the bow-drill.[1]

Unless constructed to work on a pump-drill process, as among the Iroquois Indians, the drills with a fly-wheel would not necessarily be ancestors of the top.

The Archimedean principle of propulsion is cleverly used in the colourful humming-top. Here the pumping movement gives endless pleasure, and when accompanied by its droning song can become a source of inspiration to the creative mind. It is also exploited in the schoolboy's favourite, known in my youth as the Flying Propeller (two-bladed), but today as the Flying Saucer (four-bladed).

Aspects of equilibrium, the concept of gravity and the chromatic effects which the display of optical phenomena of colours provides are a feature of most tops, whether spun on the table or on the floor.

The gyroscope is an interesting scientific development of the top idea. As a novelty it has been in its turn superseded by the most recent craze, invented by a Swede. Made from plastic, and known as the Tippy Tap, this type will turn upside down and spin on its head!

It seems that the traditional wooden tops are now a thing of the past. In an investigation on traditional games Mr. F. P. Boniface has reported that, when a boy, he used to "name them from their resemblance to vegetables." Thus, in the shop he would ask for a carrot, a turnip, a mushroom or a window-breaker. In addition to these, the nickname for the common peg-top was "a pear."

Hoops (13) were originally intended, and still are, to reinforce wine kegs or beer barrels. Then some child in the fifteenth century got hold of a loose hoop and so the trundling game began.[2] In Victorian times the old-fashioned metal hoop was controlled by a "skimmer," the vernacular name for the hook-and-handle apparatus held in the hand.

This is in contrast with the wooden, hand-made hoops more familiar to people nowadays but since 1939 extremely hard to obtain. At a television talk about traditional toys, and in response to my rhetorical question, "Now, how many of you have seen this metal type?" I received a large mail from children all over the country, with some charming letters and sketches—and one offer from a merchant offering me fifty such hoops at two shillings each!

[1] Department of Ethnography, British Museum.
[2] *Vide* Pieter Breughel's painting, *Kinderspel.*

The old craftsmen who used to steam unseasoned wood into the shape of hoops are now almost extinct. Just another instance of how necessity still mothers invention can be found in the new methods of making hoops now being followed, and occasioned by the acute shortage of pliable woods in Britain.

One such process is the use of beech veneers. These are wound four or five times round a mandrell the size of the hoop, and bonded with special glue. When dry, the cylinders thus formed are sliced into half-an-inch or five-eights-of-an-inch widths to give the finished article. This forms a laminated hoop without any pins or perceptible joins—a delight to teachers and pupils who have a good use for wooden hoops in the practice of eurythmics and dancing movements, and for ordinary athletic routines in the gymnasium.

Hoop play as an exercise for deportment was a feature of French schools for young ladies, and the following account was obtained from a woman who spent her schooldays at a Belgian convent:

"My impression is that it was part of an antique dance and should have been accompanied. Two girls faced one another at some distance apart—not fixed by any particular mark. Each had a pair of light hoop sticks, the handles of which were bound up with tinsel and coloured ribbons. Each had a light and very small hoop similarly bound. The game was to twitch the hoops off the sticks simultaneously high into the air and catch them. Once or twice a nun I did not know used to make six or more children play this, and then there were elaborate figures. But these attempts failed as no one was skilful enough to keep the hoops going, and moreover it was recognised as a hot-weather game allowing one to talk. The game was called 'les Graces'—and that is all I know. Could it have been Greek in origin, since the poses in some way were classic in conception?"

The tying of cords to parts of the body is one of the oldest methods of animating toys otherwise devoid of movement. The wooden tiger, or panther, with jaws controlled by the pulling of a string is the earliest known instance of this device (3) and has been cited in all international authorities on the subject.[1] It is Egyptian in origin, and on view at the British Museum.

The animation of wooden figures through string-pulling operations has its origins in Asiatic lands. Marionette-play and string puppetry as practised by the Javanese[2] furnish sources of contrast with our European toys and dancing mannikins; whereas the celebrated Ming Dynasty painting on silk entitled *The Hundred Children*[3] shows

[1] Gröber, Plate III; Jackson; Herčík, p. 12; C. G. Holme, *The Studio*, 1934.
[2] T. S. Raffles, *History of Java*.
[3] Prints Department, British Museum.

Chinese children working string puppets with an advanced mechanism. While dancing puppets (*poupées*), controlled by wires and strings, have always been a source of entertainment to grown-ups, it is only very recently that replicas designed specifically as children's toys have appeared in England.[1] By contrast, glove-puppets have been favourite playthings for half a century, notably the old-fashioned monkey, animated by three fingers, one inserted in its hollow head, and the other two fitting into each arm. Punch and Judy characters are less often found in glove-puppet designs, but a series of clowns and pussy-cats appear from time to time in the shops.

Folk-toys originating in Central Europe, popularised in France, and at one time common all over England, are the Pecking Chicks. These never fail to excite and delight children by their action of flitting tails and pecking beaks. The birds, or sometimes animals, carved in soft wood and pegged to a simple platform, are caused to move by the rotary action of a wooden ball suspended pendulum-wise from the centre and connected by guide-strings to each figure.

A nineteenth-century variant, made in England, of carved wood and hand-painted, is in the Bethnal Green Museum. This can be clipped to a bench or table by means of a thumb-screw. When the plumb-weight is swung the strings go into action and the neck and tail, loosely jointed, work up and down to give a vivid impression of a bird pecking at grains of corn.

An entertaining use of string is when black thread is employed to conceal the manipulation of the Dancing Skeleton toy. This simple puppet, cut out of cardboard, and jointed by pins, has its features painted with phosphorus to give an uncanny effect in the dark. The dancing action is by remote control, executed by a person holding one end of the black thread, having previously tied the other to the leg of a table or chair. The dancing skeleton had a popular forerunner in a cardboard Charlie Chaplin with turned-out boots which gyrated in response to the tightening or slackening thread.

From the string puppet derives our English Jumping Jack. A German copper-plate of 1796 showing a toy-pedlar suggests that he may have come here direct from the Continent. His representation as Merry Jack is more popular, although the finest form in which I have seen this toy is as Harlequin superbly hand-painted and carved, with pull-string weighted by a small red heart shaped from wood.[2]

[1] W. S. Lanchester, *Hand Puppets and String Puppets*.

[2] Joyce Holt Collection.

18. Washing-women: home-made pendulum-movement toy

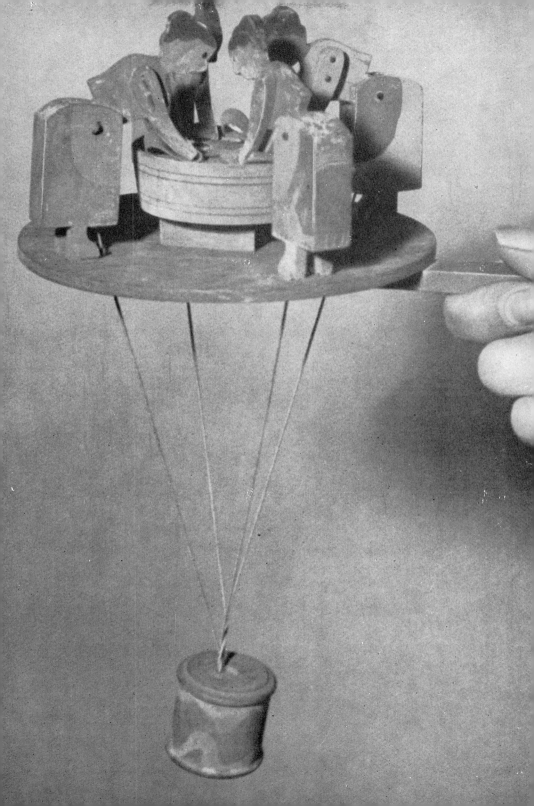

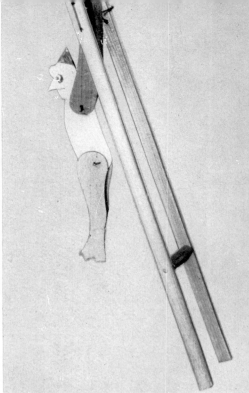

19. Wooden leverage toys: Indian hand-
    carved tiger; climbing cat by Kathleen
    Sheehan
20. Traditional Jumping Jack

The principle of torque is adroitly exploited in the instance of the jumping trapeze-man, extremely attractive in coloured wood. By squeezing the ends of the toy, in a pincer movement, the child can control at will the little fellow and so make him jump over, or swing around, the crossed cords (20).

String used for the pull-toy, as far as movement is concerned, is the complement of wheels or rollers, an aspect which will presently be considered (22, 23).

The Monkey-up-a-Stick and his companion the Admiral-up-a-Mast are both very British developments of the peasant moving animals, mostly deer or horses, made in Central Europe for generations (19). This application of leverage can be traced back to the toys of the primitive peoples of the East, who also knew how to utilise this movement for theatrical performances and shadow-play.[1]

Movement by balance and counter-balance most certainly can be traced back to the cultures of China, India and Burma, where it is still found in their balancing figures carved so beautifully from soft wood.

The most lovely of these toys is the Chinese balancing-man at the Bethnal Green Museum. A more ornamental example of the same principle was the Dancing Lady, who pirouetted on the tip of one toe aided by bullets attached to her waist by stiff rods, so that her centre of gravity was below her feet.[2]

The use of a lead weight in the balancing process is also illustrated by the familiar parrot perched on its ring, or the circus horse tilted on the edge of a shelf or table.

An older variant of this type was the man in the sailing boat who rocked in perfect security, having a stable equilibrium which never failed to reassert itself as soon as the circumstances permitted it. The centre of gravity of the vessel lay somewhere amidships. The curve of the wire was so adjusted as to bring the centre of gravity under its point of support. This seeming inconsistency in the laws of physics was a familiar children's trick, as in the bucket of water suspended from the end of a free portion of a stick partly resting on a table and projecting over the edge. The stick not being fixed or propped, one gets the impression that the bucket is hanging from no adequate support.

The lead weight is the hidden secret of the toy tumbler which keeps upright. Looking at the folk-toys of Japan, one finds a similarity in

[1] M. Medira, *Como Juegan los Niños de Todo el Mondo* (Barcelona, 1942).
[2] T. W. Erle, *Science in the Nursery*.

21. Tumbler, with weighted base, also called a "Kelly"

design between some of these ancestor-images and, the modern weighted tumblers designed as pot-bellied clowns (21).[1]

T. W. Erle makes the delightful comment that if this toy were taken as a text for a discussion on gravity it would be "strictly apropos to it, since the whole performances of a tumbler are exclusively concerned with the action of this force!"

Movement by turning a handle is a convention in the toy kingdom. Making use of the crankshaft, roller, cog-wheel, gear and other systems of wheel combination, these handle-turning toys are everywhere to be found. Whether the unique Oilcake Crusher, or Good Dog Tray, beloved of Gordon Craig; the trainer and his two dancing bears (50) (a black and a white, who are made to turn clockwise or counter-clockwise by a turn of the handle); the Swiss cardboard schoolboys who, to the sound of tinkling music, are propelled on a belting of tape up the mountain to their chalet school; these toys that do unexpected things are the true embodiments of mechanical movement in the hierarchy of a child's heart.

Toys employing the sudden change of gravity by the shifting of a weight to effect movement are designed as a series of tumblers, which fall over each other in a regulated movement down a row of steps at different levels (29).

The idea, which Mussenbroeck in his *Introductio ad philosophiam naturalem* (Leyden, 1762) ascribes to "an old invention of the Chinese," was never emulated by English toy-makers, although one example, of Austrian origin, can be seen in the Bethnal Green Collection.

The tumblers are also described by Ozanam in his *Récréations Mathématiques et Physiques*, 1694, a second edition of which appeared in 1790, edited by Montacula, with explanatory diagrams.

The shifting of balance is brought about by the movement of quicksilver. In a tube, contained within the bodies of the tumbling dolls, a small quantity of mercury flows from one end to the other as the tilting figures begin their gymnastics. The moment that this tube is inclined horizontally, the mercury flows to the lower end, thus tilting one figure over the other. The force of inertia carries it far enough to tilt the tubes again so that the mercury flows back to the opposite end. The process is repeated as long as there are steps to descend. By a very simple arrangement of pulleys, the legs and arms are always brought into suitable positions to support the figure in every position of its backward somersaults.

[1] F. Starr, *Japanese Toys.*

22. This cat's head nods when it is pulled along, *c.* 1850
23. This jigging Irishman spins round when the toy is in motion, *c.* 1850

One of the most common "penny toys" of the nineteenth century is the string-manipulated Jumping Jack. Of German origin, the toy was universally sold by pedlars on the Continent, as we can discover from old prints and engravings. Yet the dancing mannikin, whose legs and arms are made to gyrate fantastically by a simple action of a master-string, most likely derives from non-European sources, such as those patterns of Javanese puppetry and puppet-play were the conception of animating limbs by this method is first found.

The use of the coiled spring to produce sudden movement is best exemplified in the instance of the proverbial Jack-in-the-Box (24). Sometimes called by names like "Johnny Jump-ups" or "Surprise Boxes," the beginnings of this toy are obscure. The key to a sixteenth-century origin may rest in the name "Punch Boxes," for the expressions and grimaces on the oldest known papier-mâché faces have a distinct resemblance to the Polichinelle of that period.

Presumably the toy began as a sort of practical joke arising from the kind of shock and surprise that the Punch-and-Judy comedy evokes. Another form of this toy was a box from which a snake sprang up when the lid was unlatched, thus suggesting that the aim of the toy was originally to frighten rather than to give pleasure.

For the purpose of considering mechanical toys, we shall understand by the term automaton such self-moving machines as are made either in the form of men or of animals or by which animal motions and functions are to some extent imitated.

Mechanical science, next to mathematics and astronomy, was a secret jealously guarded by the philosophers and priests of antiquity. Mysterious self-moving machines were part of their stock-in-trade for working on the minds of the ignorant or the superstitious. Something analogous, in present-day terms, might be instanced where a witch-doctor of a jungle tribe utilises a modern clockwork toy, or a music-box, in his magico-ritualistic operations.

One of the earliest allusions in literature to such contraptions is in Homer's *Iliad*. Here we are told that:

> "Full twenty tripods for his hall he framed
> That placed on living wheels of massy gold
> (Wondrous to tell) instinct with spirit rolled
> From place to place, around the blessed abodes,
> Self-moved, obedient to the beck of gods." [1]

[1] Pope's translation, *Iliad*, Book XVIII.

24. English Jack-in-the-box, a surprise toy derived from Mr. Punch

There have been many later references by poets to the amazing mechanical devices of Vulcan, among which were golden statues, the representations of living maidens, which not only appeared to be endowed with lifelike qualities but which went by his side and used to support him as he walked. Aristotle also mentions self-moving tripods, and it is recorded by Philostratus that Apollonius of Tyana had seen similar pieces of mechanism among the Brahmins of India in those early days.

25. Water-wheel toy, c. 1850. The mechanism is worked by a system of pulleys, weights and cords and derives its motive power from a water-driven wheel

According to tradition, Daedalus made self-moving statues, small figures of the gods, of which Plato writes that "unless they were fastened they would of themselves run away,"[1] This he makes Socrates use as a figure of speech to illustrate the importance of not only acquiring but of holding on fast to scientific truth, that it may not fly away from us. Referring to these statues, Aristotle affirms that Daedalus accomplished his object by putting into them quicksilver.

[1] *Menos.*

The learned mechanician Bishop Wilkins points out, however, in his *Mechanical Magic* (1648) that "this would have been too grosse a way for so excellent an artificer; it is more likely that he did it with wheels and weights."

Another writer, Macrobius, tells that in the temple of Hieropolis there were moving statues.[1] A contemporary of Plato, the celebrated Pythagorean philosopher, mathematician, cosmographer and mechanician, Archytas of Tarentum, to whom are accredited the inventions of the screw and the crane, is said to have constructed a wooden pigeon that could fly about but which could not rise again once having settled. A detailed account is given by Aulus Gellius, who lived in the reigns of Trajan, Hadrian, Antoninus Pius and Marcus Aurelius. This writer records that "many men of eminence among the Greeks, and Favonius the philosopher, a most vigilant searcher into antiquity, have in a most positive manner assured us that the model of a pigeon, formed in wood by Archytas, was so contrived as by a certain mechanical art and power to fly; so nicely was it balanced by weights and put in motion by hidden and inclosed air."[2] The actual words of Favonius in this quotation are: "Archytas of Tarentum, being both a philosopher and skilled in mechanics, made a wooden pigeon, which, had it ever settled, would not have risen again till now."

Of all the early inventors the most remarkable genius was Hero of Alexandria. He lived about 150 B.C. in the reign of Ptolemy VII. From his unusual book *Epeiritalia,* a great storehouse of ingenuity, we can divide his experiments into those primarily scientific and those intended to give to their owners some of the more delectable refinements of playing with toys. (To the former belong the first siphon in both its typical forms; the syringe; the well-known portable shower-bath; the clack valve; the fire-engine with an air vessel for ensuring a continuous stream; the self-trimming lamp; the steam blow pipe; the pneumatic fountain; the steam-engine; the penny-in-the-slot automatic machine for obtaining a drink or a charge of perfume.)

The earliest example of Hero's work in toy-making was a bird which, by means of a stream of water, was made to pipe or sing (26). This diminutive automaton consisted of a pedestal, which was in reality a watertight tank fitted with a funnel, the stem of which reached nearly to the bottom. To the right of the funnel was a little

[1] *Saturnaliorum Conviviorum.*
[2] *Noctes Attica.*

artificial shrub, on which sat a bird. A tube led up from the roof of the tank and terminated in a little whistle, the end of which dipped into a cup containing water. When water was poured into the funnel the air in the tank was driven out through the tube and whistle. Bubbling up through the water in this way came a sound as if the bird was singing. This device, dating back to a century and a half before Christ, is the ancestor of the well-known bubbling bird-whistle toy as we know it now.

26. Hero's Singing Bird   27. Hero's use of heat to produce movement

From C. W. Cooke's "Automata Old and New," 1891

A second example was more complicated. It featured an elaborate arrangement of four small birds being watched by an owl. The moment the owl's back was turned the birds began to sing, but ceased again as soon as he turned towards them. In this apparatus the birds are made to sing in the same way as in the previous toy, *i.e.* by the displacement of air in the tank, but as soon as the level of the water in the tank reaches the top of a concentric siphon the water is discharged into a bucket. Then the birds stop singing, and the bucket, because of its added weight, lifts a counterbalance weight. In so doing it turns the spindle which supports the owl. When the bucket is full its contents are discharged by a small siphon inside. It is drawn up by an affixed weight; the owl turns its back to the birds, and the cycle of operations is repeated.

Another Hero mechanical toy was even more elaborate. It has a pedestal upon which were constructed four small bushes, each having a bird perched among its branches. When water was allowed to flow into the funnel the first bird began to whistle. After a few minutes it left off, when the next bird would begin. When it had finished the third sang, then the fourth, and back to the first, in a continuous series just as long as water flowed into the funnel. From the diagrams which accompany the Italian edition, published at Urbino in 1592 (Alessandro Georgi's translation) and from the Amsterdam version of 1680, we get some impression of the simple manner by which Hero achieved his effects. These were produced by a combination of as many superposed tanks as there were birds to sing, the one emptying into the other by siphons.

Having achieved perfection with his device of continuous mechanical singing, he was next urged to experiment with intermittent sound. In this he succeeded by making the water flow into a little cup which toppled over, the minute it was full, and emptied itself into the funnel. Being loaded at the bottom, it would then immediately right itself, and the sound was produced by displaced air escaping through a whistle in the manner already described.

Not all the models created by Hero were operated by the action of water. He also exploited heat to obtain an increase in air pressure whereby certain automatic actions were produced. Characteristic of this heat action was a metal ornament representing a priest on one side, and a priestess on the other, officiating at an altar (27). The effect when the fire on the altar was lit made the two figures pour libations on to the sacrifice. The altar was in the form of an airtight metallic box which communicated by means of a central tube with a larger box forming the pedestal. Into this lower reservoir wine or other liquid was poured through a hole in the base. When the fire was lighted the air in the altar-box expanded and, pressing on the surface of the liquid in the pedestal, forced some of it through the tubes passing through the body and down the right arm of each figure.

One of Hero's most interesting mechanical effects showed a combination of hydraulic, pneumatic and mechanical actions. It is a figure of Hercules armed with a bow and arrow. There is also a dragon lying under an apple tree, from which an apple has fallen to the ground. When the apple is lifted Hercules shoots his arrow at the dragon, which begins to hiss and continues to make this ominous noise for some minutes. The illustration (28) shows how the apparatus was worked by a double tank connected by a valve, which is in turn attached to the apple by a cord. Another cord passed over a pulley and connected the apple with a trigger in Hercules' right hand. Upon lifting the apple, the trigger was released, and at the same time the valve opened, permitting the water in the upper tank to flow into the lower. By this means air was forced through a tube into the dragon's mouth, emitting the hissing sound which continued until the upper tank emptied itself of liquid.

Others of Hero's famous automata consisted of a model of Vulcan's workshops in which a smith assisted by three hammermen forges a

28. Hercules and the Dragon. *From C. W. Cooke's "Automata Old and New,"* 1891

piece of iron, all working in synchronised movement; a bird which not only makes a noise but at certain times will drink any liquid presented to it; a figure so constructed on a system of wheels and cogs that when a knife is passed between the head and the body the head is not severed—not only this, but the figure can actually drink before and after the operation.

For nearly a thousand years after Hero little advance in mechanical toys is recorded. During the Dark Ages, when credulity and ignorance were rife, greatly exaggerated accounts of mechanicals were passed on by word of mouth. Hero's scientific discoveries were forgotten, and it was not until the first Latin edition of his *Epeiritalia* published by Commandinus in Italy in 1575 that inquiring minds began to re-examine his advanced discoveries, which had been lost sight of.

In the interim, fabulous automata were apparently used in connection with the folk-festivals of the Middle Ages which retained a semi-pagan character. Magic toys were, of course, discouraged by the clergy, who condemned in severe terms any artisan who happened to sell his inventions to unauthorised persons, lest it fall into the hands of the laity.

In 1086 it is on record that "benediction was refused to one of the candidates for the noviciate for that he is said to be a mechanician and a necromancer." Speaking heads of brass and wood were anathema to churchmen, and St. Thomas Aquinas energetically rooted them out wherever he could, and smashed them.

In England Oliver Cromwell was no more indulgent towards the giant automatic toys designed to amuse the Stuart kings, castigating these, in his puritanical wrath, as "monsters."

The sixteenth century found Baldi, a mathematician, applying some of Hero's hydraulic principles to move parts of mechanical figures and to make an eagle fly. A rising interest in such wonders as were being witnessed on the Continent of Europe was reflected in travellers' tales, the rumoured feats of alchemists, and the popularity of stories curious and fantastical which were then getting into print. In 1635 John Bate published under the title of *The Mysteries of Nature and Art*, a collection of unusual devices which were nothing more than inaccurate re-hashes of the Italian editions of Hero's works. A few years later, in 1659, there appeared another curious book by Isaac de Caus, on water-works, and covering much the same ground. Entitled *New and Rare Inventions of Water Workers*, it was first written in French, and purports to describe "Perpetual Motion, many hard labours performed and variety of Motions of Sounds produced."

In 1697 appeared a *Compleat History of the Most Remarkable Providences that have happened in this Present Age*, by William Turner. At the end of the volume there is a supplement entitled "Artificial Knick-knacks, Projects, Curiosities," which reveals a contemporary interest in such subjects as the early mechanical toys. The compiler explains his object thus:

"I shall present to my reader here, an Epitome of Artifices, a Miscellany Compendium of little pretty fancies and curiosities, like the webs of the silkworm, or Spider of an ingenuous texture and Contrivance, enough to demonstrate the finesse of Man's wit."

This texture and finesse he exemplified by quotations from the classics and from contemporary sources like *Dr. Brown's Travels*, *The History of the Manual Arts* and Gafferet's *Unheard of Curiosities*. From the latter he cites the following passage:

"I shall also omit to speak of the Inventions of divers Hydraulicks in our own times, which are of so wonderful strange contrivance, as that there is no thing in the World that they do not imitate; as also those Statues of Men and Women that speak though inarticulately; that move of themselves and play upon diverse Instruments; of Birds that fly and sing; of Lions that roar; of Dogs that bark, and others that fight with cats; in the very same manner as living Dogs do, and a thousand other wonderful Inventions of Man, which are enough to astonish our senses."

Furthermore, such references to Dresden and Nuremberg as are made in this English Chronicle have special significance in that we here have an anticipation of where the great toy-manufacturing centres of Europe were to begin to develop a century afterwards:

"I shall also pass by Architas, his wooden fly and eagle, which have in our days been made to fly at Norimberg; the author whereof has also made admirable Hydraulics and a perpetual rainbow, as Antonius Possivinus reports."

Again:

"Among the Rarities of Dresden are to be seen castles of Gold, and Mother of Pearl, many fowls and cups made of shells, a fine ostrich made out of its egg, with the feathers of gold; a cup made out of the Ball taken out of an ox's stomach, richly set, about a foot long; a hundred and twenty-one heads carved on the outside of a cherrystone; a Fryer of Japan carved in box; a glass organ, etc. . . ."

Toy miniatures seemed to hold a strong fascination for the compiler of this strange compendium, for his favourite quotation is a reference from Pliny:

"Myrmecides wrought out of ivory, a chariot with four wheels and so many horses, in so little room that a little fly might cover them with her wings. The same man made a ship, with all the tackling to it, no bigger than a small bee might hide it with her wings."

It was in Nuremberg in the year 1672 that there occurred an historical turning-point in the evolution of automatic control, for then two local craftsmen named Hautch were employed to make performing soldiers of silver for the child of Louis XIV.[1]

From then onwards, throughout the whole eighteenth century, the initiative in developing clockwork toys of particularly high artistry

[1] Karl Gröber, *Children's Toys of Bygone Days*, p. 17.

seems to have gone to the French. In France, that pioneering spirit was maintained, enhanced by the device of musical accompaniment which went into all the Royal nurseries (and many of the aristocratic playrooms) of East and West. It continued until a century later when clockwork, or spring-operated, units were mass-produced everywhere in toy manufacture, and France had to compete with Germany, England, America and Japan in the making of cheaper clockwork toys of tin.

The outstanding name in this era of French mechanical toys was that of Jacques Vaucanson.[1] He turned out his models from 1707 to 1782, his workmanship later inspiring his countryman Pierre Jaquet-Droz. Three of Vaucanson's automata were reproduced as illustrations to an English translation of his 1738 *Memoir*. This was published in London in 1742 with the information that it was "sold at the long room at the Opera House in the Haymarket, where the mechanical figures are to be seen at 1, 2, 5, and 7 o'clock in the afternoon."

The first of these was an automatic flute-player. A wooden figure six feet six inches in height, it represented a well-known classical statue of a faun, sitting on a rock and mounted on a square stand four feet six inches from the ground. It was capable of performing twelve different pieces of music on a German flute, the instrument being played as a man would play it, by blowing across the embouchure and projecting the air with variable force by movable lips. The lips imitated in their movements those of a living player employing a tongue to regulate the opening and producing the notes by the tips of the fingers closing or opening the holes.

The mechanical principles were scientifically thought out. Within the pedestal was a train of wheel-work driven by a weight. This set into motion a small shaft on which were six cranks disposed at equal angular distances around it. Six pairs of bellows were attached to the cranks, their inlet valves being mechanically opened and closed so as to make them silent in action. The air supplied by these bellows was conveyed to three different wind-chests. One was loaded with a weight of four pounds, one with two, and the third having only the weight of its upper board. These wind-chests communicated with three small chambers in the body of the figure, and these chambers were all connected with a windpipe which passed up the throat to the cavity of the mouth and ended in the two movable lips. These

[1] C. W. Cooke, *Automata Old and New*, 1891.

between them formed an orifice and might be further modified by the action of the tongue.

The train of wheels also set into motion a cylinder two and a half feet long and twenty inches in diameter. To this were fixed a number of brass bars of different lengths and thicknesses. They in their revolution acted upon a row of fifteen keys or levers. Three of these corresponded to the three small wind-chambers containing air at different pressures, and by means of chains operated their respective valves. There were seven levers set apart for operating the fingers, their respective chains making bends at the shoulders and elbows of the automaton. They terminated at the wrist in the ends of metacarpal levers attached to the fingers, which in order to resemble the natural flesh of the hand were covered with skin. The motion of the mouth was controlled by four of the levers: one to open the lips so as to give a greater force to the wind; one to bring them closer together and so contract the passage; a third to draw the lips towards and away from the flute; and the fourth to push them forward over the edge of the embouchure.

The last of the fifteen levers was the most cleverly employed. It had the power of controlling the tongue. The barrel worked upon a screwed bearing, so that in its revolution all the levers described a spiral line sixty-four inches long. Since the barrel during the performances made twelve revolutions, it followed that the levers passed over a distance of seven hundred and sixty-eight inches in going through the twelve-tune range.

Companion piece to the automatic flute-player was a figure which played on a shepherd's pipe with one hand, while it beat a drum with the other. The instrument was a diminutive pipe with only three holes. And every note, no matter how rapid was the succession, had to be modified by the tongue. In this machine there were provided as many different pressures of air as there were notes to be sounded. It is a mechanism involving intricate fingering of the keys, which singles out its inventor from others of that period as a very remarkable man.

But of these three the most distinctive was the centre-piece. On this central pedestal stood Vaucanson's celebrated model of a duck. This he himself described in a letter to the Abbé de la Fontaine in 1738. According to the inventor, the duck demonstrated a profound physiological and anatomical knowledge and mechanical skill, for in it the operations of eating, drinking and digestion were closely imitated. The bird would stretch out its neck to take corn from the hand.

This was swallowed and discharged in a digested condition, by a process of dissolution, not trituration. In his epistle he wrote:

"I do not pretend to give this as a perfect *digestion,* capable of producing blood and nutritive particles for the support of the animal. I hope nobody will be so unkind as to upbraid me with pretending to any such thing. The matter digested in the stomach is conducted by pipes (as in an animal by the guts), quite to the anus where is a sphincter that lets it out. I pretend only to imitate the mechanism of their action in these things, *i.e.* first to swallow the corn; secondly macerate or dissolve it; thirdly to make it come out, sensibly changed from what it was."

Besides being equipped with a fantastic digestive system, every bone of the duck's wings was an exact anatomical replica. After having been wound up, the duck ate and drank; dabbled in the water with its bill; made a "gurgling" sound; flapped its wings and preened its feathers—all in one winding.

The Vaucanson duck, which drew astonished visitors to the Opera House of London's Haymarket, has its poignant dénouement. In 1840 it was discovered hidden away in a Berlin attic, very much in a state of disrepair. Then a mechanician by the name of George Tiets undertook to repair it. He had it taken to Paris, and in 1844 it was exhibited in the Place du Palais Royal. During the exhibition one of the wings became disarranged, and it was put into the hands of Robert-Houdin for repairs. Robert-Houdin took advantage of this opportunity to examine the famous digestive system, and described its action thus:

"On présentait à l'animal un vase dans lequel était de la graine baignant dans l'eau. Le movement que faisait le bec en facilitait l'introduction dans un tuyau, place sous le ventre de l'automate, laquelle se vidait toutes les trois ou quatre séances. L'évacuation était chose preparée à l'avance; une éspèce de bouillie, composée de mie de pain colorée de vert, était poussée par un coup de pompe et soigneusement réçue, sur un plateau en argent, comme produit d'une digestion artificielle."

Thus mystification yielded to the commonplace, when, like the conjurer's trick, its intricacies were exposed. In a way Vaucanson's eating and drinking duck was anticipated by the Compte de Gennes, Governor of the Island of Saint Christophe. He, according to Père Labat, had peviously constructed a peacock which could walk about the grounds, picking up corn, and would swallow and digest the grains. Vaucanson possibly had precursors: he certainly had imitators. Some of his finest pieces were given as a collection to Marie Antoinette, being described in detail by Larousse in his *Encyclopaedia* of 1841. One of his contemporaries, François Camos, interested in toymaking, wrote a treatise in 1722 on motive forces. By 1752 Du

Moulin, a silversmith, was travelling all over Europe with automata copied from Vaucanson's. These were afterwards purchased in Nuremberg by Bereis, a councillor of Helmstadt, at whose residence they were viewed in 1764 by Beckmann. The latter, in his *History of Inventions*, observes that these automata finally found their way to St. Petersburg, and that he had seen them there at the Palace of Zarsko-Selo, where he was told that they had been bought from their inventor but were not at the time in working order.

Meanwhile a zest was growing in Europe for automata that reflected with increasing ingenuity the marriage of scientific discovery to an innate desire among men to see emerging from the wheels and pulleys an impeccable robot. In this mounting curve of enthusiasm landmarks were the writing automaton which Fredrich von Knaus exhibited in Vienna in 1760; and the clock made by Le Droze of Neufchâtel for the King of Spain, and on which, besides the usual moving figure, were placed a sheep that bleated and a dog mounting guard over a basket of fruit. When the basket was touched the dog would bark and growl until it was restored. Another celebrated exhibit which toured the courts of Europe was the automatic chess-player, dressed as a life-sized Turk, which Baron Wolfgang von Kempelen constructed in 1776. Having thrilled spectators in Riga, Moscow, St. Petersburg, Berlin, Presburg and Vienna, it was brought to London in 1783, without its secret being discovered. Six years later a book was published in Dresden in which the writer claimed that "a well taught boy, very thin and tall for his age (sufficiently so that he could be concealed in a drawer below the chess-board) agitated the whole."

An attempt to satisfy the English public appetite for such mechanical inventiveness was organised in 1772 in a place of entertainment in Spring Gardens, Charing Cross, known as Cox's Museum. The descriptive catalogue refers to the "several superb and magnificent pieces of mechanism" and adds a footnote announcing: "Hours of Admission 11, 2 and 7 every day (Sundays excepted), tickets Half a Guinea each, admitting one person, to be had at Mr. Cox's, No. 103, Shoe Lane."

The articles exhibited included more than twenty large and elaborate automata, several adorned with gold and precious stones. Some were complicated clocks. Others were large groups of animals, and figures with fountains and cascades around them. Some were as high as sixteen feet, none less than nine.

James Cox for many years executed commissions for the British

29. An oriental acrobat, *c.* 1790. The figure somersaults backwards and downwards through three levels, as its centre of gravity is changed by the shifting weight of mercury concealed in the body

30. Early American fire-engine of heavy cast-iron
31. English four-seater motor-car, *c.* 1900. Height $5\frac{3}{8}$ in.

East India Company, who presented some of his amazing clocks to oriental potentates. Most of his automata went to China, where several specimens are in the Imperial Museum, Peiping. One of the most intricate and splendid examples of his clockmaker's art is owned by the Berry-Hill Corporation of America, by whose courtesy the following description is given:

"This English automatic musical clock is signed by James Cox and dated 1762. It is approximately four feet high, entirely of gilt bronze. It is built up in fanciful style, in the European-Oriental manner, supported on four winged dragons with heads upturned. The superstructure follows European lines except for the three canopies enclosing the Striking Jacks, which are Oriental in design. The Striking Jacks are clothed in Eastern costume. The oval mirror surmounting the clock is European.

"The mechanical scene is disclosed at the opening of two glass-panelled doors. The frieze clearly shows English influence, being composed alternately of the Rose of England and the Thistle of Scotland. The automatic scene is one of the most remarkable ever built by Cox. It consists of a flowing river simulated by spiral tubes. Moving along the river, to the accompaniment of music, are a succession of pleasure-boats of different types, with waterfowl at intervals. The river flows below a six-arched bridge, on which are situated rows of moving figures of ladies and gentlemen in gay contemporary dress. A number of animals complete the figures which are set to a background of a painted landscape, with a central section of pierced foliage veiling an eight-column waterfall in play.

"The musical action plays four different tunes, all popular at the time. The movement is of exceptional quality and is so contrived that is strikes the hours, and the quarters, one of the tunes being played in full at the hours. A change action alters the tune at will, and an attachment enables the music to be repeated independently of the hour whenever desired."

It was indicative of James Cox, whom Baillie described as "a very able maker," that he prefaced the Catalogue of his Spring Gardens spectacle where these works were on show with a quotation from Hipparch: "Arts," he wrote, "are of all things the most conducive to the well-being of Man; War, and the changes of Fortune may have power over everything else, but the Arts are imperishable."

The success of the Cox Exhibition created a taste for the incredible, which later was catered for by the Great Exhibition of 1851. There, rivalling the Koh-i-nor diamond in its popular appeal, was a gold snuff-box about four and a half by three inches in size. This was the workmanship of the younger Le Droze, who lived in Geneva. The action was delicately controlled, so that when a spring was touched there flew open a small door and out sprang a beautifully modelled bird, of green-enamelled gold, as fragile as a humming-bird. Through mechanical movement this bird fluttered its wings and tail, while its beak opened and shut in time to the trilling of a realistic song.

Several examples of these boxes are among the Steiner collection of mechanicals. The fact that the Swiss have come to occupy a leading place in the making of clockwork musical toys (according to H. D. Steiner, who has made a study of this subject) results from a bold attempt to take away the international trade which England had enjoyed as a country turning out superb watches and clocks. They employed various tactics in issuing this challenge. They did not succeed in winning a foremost place for their nation as watchmakers until they had installed a musical movement into their productions. It was thus that the science of horology came to be associated with the history of the mechanical toy equipped with a musical unit.

The invention of repeating (striking) work in clocks is attributed to an Englishman, Barlow, in 1676, according to Denham's *Artificial Clockmaker* of 1734. At the end of the reign of James II Barlow employed the celebrated Thomas Tompion to apply the invention to watches, but failed utterly to get a patent on the new art thus produced. The reason given for denying the Royal Patent was "same now being made by several Clockmakers. Whereof all persons concerned are to take due notice." At this time a monopoly was held on the making of clocks and watches in England by royal decree vested in the Worshipful Company of Clockmakers.

By 1789 Louis Breguet, one of the greatest watchmakers known, devised the compact wire gong for the repeating watch. This was a hard steel wire, ending in a block which was screwed to the edge of the watch plate, the wire curling round the edge of the watch and occupying only very little space.

Besides the early snuff-box type of musical box, the Swiss made the cranktype (Manivelles) box, in which the mechanism is operated by a worm screw on a cylinder wheel turned by a hand-crank. These were designed specifically for children's toys, having a simpler mechanism devoid of either spring or escapement.

Like the inventor of the mechanical spring-motor, the first Swiss maker to fit music-work into a timepiece is unknown. According to the files in the Swiss Office for the Development of Trade "the invention of the music-box dates back to the beginning of the eighteenth century, to one Louis Favre."[1] An historian, L. G. Jaccard, in a manuscript filed at the Edison Institute in America, writes:

[1] Roy Mosoriak, *The Curious History of Musical Boxes*, p. 22, Illustrations.

32. French automaton. Jumeau china dolls, which play zither and mandoline to music-box action, *c.* 1845–50

33. Erratic-movement clockwork quacking duck, German, *c.* 1900
34. Wooden horse-on-wheels; English, late eighteenth century

"The musical box has its place of origin in the Valle de Jouz, Switzerland, near the French border. In 1789 an inventory was taken in Geneva which reveals that small musical bottles and watches were then already made, which could play two airs. In 1802 Isaac Piguet replaced the watch-movements of a ring with musical works. The development of the musical box took place in two places secretly."

Jaccard also mentions an old report of an exposition at which "one Salomon Favre was the first to introduce music devices into watches."

When towards the end of the nineteenth century the Swiss had perfected an eight-tune, pin-cylinder type, key-wound unit, they installed it in a hand-carved armchair suitable for a small child to sit in. The musical chair was a well-finished article, usually hand-carved in walnut. It became a much-sought-after piece of nursery furniture. When the child sat on thes eat the resultant pressure released a large spring which set off the works inside. When the child got up the music stopped. One tune followed another until the spring-motor ran down. A push-rod could be operated to stop the music at a given moment.

The French showed a special aptitude for making amusing and original musical moving figures, during the nineteenth century. Some of these represented caricatures of courtiers in formal costume, with the heads of monkeys. One, for example, admires himself effeminately in a mirror, turning his head approvingly from side to side; another model takes snuff; a third delicately balances a cigarette-holder between his finger and thumb which, when a cigarette has been inserted in it and lit, he places between his lips and by a suction movement actually draws out smoke which then issues from the mouth and nostrils. Woolly and human-like hair is a feature of these macabre mechanical figures.

Many of the French designs are in the form of negro servants about two inches high carrying trays of fruit or surprise items. One is a female servant with three coconut shells set on her tray. As the mechanism starts up her head nods in wonderment, and the pupils of her eyes shift sideways. Then the shell on the right lifts up to music and a monkey's head is shown moving from left to right and mimicking human chatter with its lips. The second shell reveals a pirouetting ballerina who dances to a lively tune; while her shell cover is still raised, the third is upraised to disclose a waltzing mouse, which moves fantastically in circles to appropriate music. The entire drama lasts for three and a half minutes with one winding.

Examples of these rare mechanical toys are in the H. D. Steiner Collection in London. Here also is a French musical toy in the form of a period doll sitting at an upright piano. As the music plays, concealed within the piano case, the player turns her head and her hands move over the keys. Perhaps the example in this collection most suitable for children is a hand-operated musical box portraying the "Kitten's Tea-Party," of German manufacture. A group of kittens sit round a table placed on the lid of the cabinet, realistically clothed in fur, and go through the movements of drinking tea while the handle simultaneously churns out a pretty melody.

A similar tableau, in an American collection,[1] features six dolls, a rocking-horse and a dog with a ball, all with movement. Two dolls sit at a table playing cards; one sips tea alone; the scene is built on a stage twenty-six inches wide, which holds the musical unit in its base, playing four tunes. Other European variants now in American collections number a musical merry-go-round with dolls in the swings; another, with riders seated on horses and picturesque conveyances which move around in a circle, while crank-action makes music; a polar-bear whose head turns as the ball balanced on his snout revolves; a street barrel-organ with a lady playing cymbals; a man with a pack on his back which he opens up to disclose figures like dogs peeping out.

Whereas grandiose constructions, in the Vaucanson or Maillardet traditions, could be enjoyed only by the privileged classes, a popular demand grew up for toys of this kind which came within the incomes of the general public. The demand was answered by a French sailor, called Cruchet, who fought at Trafalgar.[2] He simplified the ornate toys, and thus put on the market the first precursors of the cheap clockwork toys that later came from the factories of Nuremberg and Fürth, winning between 1850 and 1900 a reputation for the German toy trade in every other country (71).

Napoleon is said to have bought hundreds of cheap mechanical toys which were distributed by the Empress Josephine to war-widows who came to the Palace to beg for a pension. Very few of these clockwork toys of the First Empire are still extant. Some are preserved in the Musée de l'Armée in Paris; others at the Musée du Canavalet.

---

[1] Roy Mosoriak, *The Curious History of Musical Boxes,* p. 166; and Eleanor St. George, *Dolls of Three Centuries,* pp. 1–10, Jumeau Musical Dolls (Sribner's 1951).

[2] L. and R. Freeman, *Cavalcade of Toys,* p. 184.

At a Munich museum there is a coach with six horses and postillions. The Nuremberg Museum has, among others, a mechanical canal boat. Several Nuremberg toys found their way to the Royal Nursery where Queen Victoria played as a princess. One in particular was described by Mrs. Jackson,[1] who examined it closely at Kensington Palace. It was a hand-loom about twenty-two inches in length, on which jute is being woven into a coarse cloth. A second favourite was a miniature tree-planted roadway, on which a two-and-a-half-inch figure of a little doll moves along grooved lines; two of these run parallel; a small pagoda-shaped building at either end partly conceals the action of the puppet as it turns into the path parallel with the one just traversed. According to Mrs. Jackson, the greatest favourite with the Queen consisted of a miniature stage about eight inches long and three wide. On this three figures, brilliantly dressed in silks and satins, danced and pirouetted in a most animated and laughable manner to the music of a little musical-box concealed beneath the stage. The whole was enclosed in a neat little rosewood box in the shape of an upright piano. There was a leather strap for suspension round the neck of the little royal owner when she was "playing at being showman."

Motive power from vulcanised india-rubber was introduced into toys in France about 1878. It gripped the popular imagination when applied to mechanical butterflies sold by the street-traders of Paris. A light screw propeller or fan rotated by the untwisting of a spring, while two fixed wings or fins were set on the body of the insect to prevent the whole thing from rotating. With bat-like flight these mechanical toys would fill the air of the Avenue de l'Opéra. The same principle was followed in the manufacture of a running mouse. It was especially interesting from the fact that the machine wound itself up from the moment the tension of the cord was relaxed. As the spindle of the wheels was made of flexible rubber the realistic scuttling action of a mouse was well imitated.

There followed a wide variety of mechanical toys in which the rubber sping principle was combined with a wheel and escapement, the pallets of which by their reciprocating motion produced any desired effect. Typical was the swimming fish, the wagging of whose tail was produced in this way. Another was a pair of boxers whose arms hung loosely from the shoulders by rubber hinges. An escapement

[1] *Toys of Other Days.*

wheel worked a crutch, which, by a pair of cranks linked together, caused each of the two pugilists to turn a little way backwards and forwards on one heel, giving the appearance of hitting out vigorously.

Patents registered at this period included bucking mules (1874), mechanical chariots (1875), bucking horses (1885), and Punch and Judy (1892).[1]

The flywheel principle was also utilised to the fullest at this time. One English adaptation of it was in the form of an ostrich yoked to a two-wheel cart. The effect of the birds' strut was delightfully reproduced, and it appeared to be drawing the cart, whereas the movement in reality pushed the ostrich along.

The great attraction in London at the beginning of the clockwork epoch was a display of mechanical toys put on by a Frenchman in the same place where Cox had shown his wonders. His name was Maillardet and the *pièce de résistance* in his collection was a mechanical bird whose performance lasted four minutes with one winding-up. He also constructed a spider, entirely of steel, which imitated all the actions of a living insect. It ran around and around in a spiral line, tending towards the centre. Other outstanding automata made by Maillardet represented a caterpillar, a mouse, a lizard and a serpent. The last darted about all over the table, shot in and out its fang and produced a hissing noise.

This exhibition is remembered most for Maillardet's drawing-and-writing figure and his famous pianoforte-player. The former was a kneeling boy who wrote in ink with an ordinary pen, phrases in both English and French. He also drew landscapes. The latter was the figure of a lady who could perform eighteen separate pieces of music. Her performance began with a bowing movement to the audience; her bosom heaved; her eyes looked first at the musical score, then followed the motion of her fingers along the miniature keyboard. As the fingers struck individual notes the music synchronised with them.

Another master of mechanical construction was Robert-Houdin, whose achievements included a toy confectioner's shop, in which a pastry-cook came out of the door when requested and offered cakes, bonbons and all kinds of refreshments. Within the shop could be seen the assistants in the acts of rolling out dough, shaping the pastry, and putting the tins into the oven. Another of his inventions was an acrobat which performed tricks on a trapeze. His most famous was

[1] *Cavalcade of Toys*, p. 186.

35. The Drinking Bear, transition between lavish automata and popular clockwork toys

undoubtedly a couple of circus clowns, called Auriol and Debureau respectively. Auriol went through complicated acrobatic feats on a chair which was held at arm's length by his partner. He would then smoke a pipe, and while the circus orchestra played an air he accompanied on the flageolet.

Music became an indispensable attraction of thee mechanical toys and one of Robert-Houdin's contemporaries, one M. Mareppe, is said to have constructed a very wonderful automatic violin-player, shown at the Conservatoire de Paris in 1838, whose musical execution was so moving, and whose fingering of the strings so lifelike, that spectators wept from emotion.

But such accomplishments as Mareppe's were exceptional. At this time the perfecting of musical boxes was still in its very early stages, and they had not yet been put on the market as a child's toy, either spring-wound or handle-operated. In 1830 the musical range was confined to a primitive double-squeak, with only a small volume of sound being emitted. The technical problem confronting designers was to increase the volume of sound and range of tone. This led in 1833 to the large-sized musical box, known as "the cartel," being offered at Geneva. The cartel evolved rapidly with such improvements as "the mandoline note" and a modulated model in two sections which could play loudly or softly as the musical composition demanded. This was known as the "forte-piano" type. Jaccard, in his accounts of this development, refers to the introduction of drums, bells and castanets, at first arranged in full view behind the cylinder, and latterly concealed under the bed-plates. By 1850 the effect of flute-music was added. The next phase was the most expensive one, combining comb-music as in the original types with air-vibrated reeds. Refinements reached their high-point with the addition of wooden or metal whistles, giving an orchestral quality to the reproduction, and the name "orchestra" to the cabinets. For the next forty years the fine tone and clear bell-like quality of the music were maintained. The movements were fitted into chime-toys which produced a short tune by rolling a wheel along the floor.

36. Clockwork-operated monkey, *c.* 1900. When wound up, he beats the toy drum rhythmically. Height 18 in.

IV

TOYS THAT MOVE—II

I T was not until about 1900 that the English toy industry really began to make any headway against German predominance. About 1880 the firm of W. Britain and Sons, famous today as producers of toy soldiers, set up in business by putting on the market some original toys in competition with the Continental range.

37. The Mechanical Foot Race

A contemporary catalogue contains descriptive information about each toy, together with expressive drawings in line. Of the items listed, nine examples have survived the perils and breakages that toys are heir to. The following excerpts are of historic interest, since they indicate what appealed to the young mind of that period as well as the construction and design of British-made toys driven by clockwork.

"The justly celebrated Automatic Walking Match consists of a handsomely got-up stand designed to represent a tent round which two men (nine inches in height), richly dressed in silk and satin, are made to walk rapidly, and pass and re-pass one another in such a manner that it is quite impossible for anyone to predict which will be the winner at the close of a predetermined number of rounds. The action of the men's legs is quite natural, in fact a fair toe-and-heel race (37).

"The handsome white Poodle, that runs about or stands still at will, and forms a most interesting and amusing present for a child, being strongly made and not likely to get out of order; goes by clockwork and is also capable of carrying any little figure on its back, such as a doll (38).

38. The Mechanical Dog   39. The Mechanical Bear

"The Bear (39) is similar to the Mechanical Dog, but in addition to running along, it lifts its head up and down, and moves from side to side, opening and shutting its mouth, and showing its teeth all the while in a most savage manner.

"The Highlander is larger but on the same principle as the Chinaman. He stands sixteen inches in height, and is dressed in velvet coat, plaid, kilt, shawl, etc., and moves both arms. In his right hand he holds a bottle, and in his left a glass. He first pours out a glassful from the bottle, and then drinks it off, throwing his head back at the same time. This movement also goes for about half-an-hour with one winding (40).

"The Chinese Mandarin is a very clever and pleasing mechanical figure, richly dressed in satin and gold lace, and stands twelve inches in height. In his right hand he holds a cup, and in his left a saucer. On winding up the figure he will raise the cup to his mouth and, after first tasting, will drink with evident satisfaction. It is very strongly made and will go for half-an-hour with one winding. This figure has achieved great success as a window attraction for shops, particularly grocery stores (41).

40. The Highlander   41. The Tea-drinking Chinaman

"The strongly made smoking figure of the Khedive (42) goes by clockwork, and smokes cigarettes or a pipe in the most natural manner possible, puffing out the smoke in clouds; and being made on a new principle without valves, is not likely to clog with the juice from the tobacco or herbs which it may have to smoke. Handsomely got up, and sitting on a carpeted box, it forms a novel and attractive present, or if introduced at Christmas parties, is sure to excite much admiration and cause considerable amusement.

"The performer of the well-known Basket Trick (43). This represents a turbaned Indian, one and a half times as big in proportion as the Khedive, sitting on a box, handsomely covered in silk plush, with a basket in front of him, holding in his right hand a wand, and in his left the basket lid. On winding the figure up he proceeds to tap

42. The Khedive   43. The Indian Juggler

on the top of the basket with his wand, after which he raises
the basket lid and a child is found sitting in the basket; after a while
he re-covers the basket with the lid, taps again with his wand, raises
the lid, and to the surprise and astonishment of everyone, the child
is transposed into a horrid-looking snake, and so on through a number
of changes.

"The old story of Don Quixote and the Windmill is illustrated in a
pleasing toy (44) representing a knight clad in armour, and mounted on
horseback, who gallops round and attacks a gaily-coloured windmill
with his lance. This forms an amusing game by counting the number
of times, or the different coloured fans of the mill he strikes, each
player having chosen his colour beforehand.

"The toy Equestrienne (45) consists of a horse galloping round a ring
as at a circus. Standing upon the back of the horse is a fairy who, as the
horse passes under the bar, stoops and then jumps, clearing the bar
in a most clever manner, alighting upon the horse's back and stands,
balancing herself until the horse reaches the bar, when she again
jumps, continuing to ride and jump until the horse stops.

"The very elegant Fountain Top is wound up and spun in the ordinary way, but instead of placing it on the table it is stood in a saucerful
of water. It immediately throws up a magnificent jet of water, varying
in height according to the strength of the spinner (46).

"The Mikadoisan ornament for the mantelshelf is always amusing.
When the umbrella is spun the figure vigorously fan himself with
the fan that he holds in his left hand (47).

44. Don Quixote and the Windmill

45. The Equestrienne

"The Horse Race consits of a stand supporting two jockeys on horses who, when the race is started, race round and round, passing and re-passing one another in such a manner that it is positively impossible to tell which will win until the race is over. With this game children can be kept amused for hours (48).

"The figure of a Soldier mounted on a hobby-horse carries an umbrella over his shoulder which, when it is set spinning, causes the soldier to run rapidly along and to use his sword vigorously as he goes (49)."

Other excellent examples of these early English clockwork toys are in the Percy Muir Collection, notably a metal motor-car of *c.* 1910; Chinese laundrymen who toss their comrade in a blanket; and a walking doll which, when wound by a key, steps along the floor in measured paces.

In all the early clockwork toys the gears were arranged so that uncoiling of the spring operated the mechanism, making the object move along the floor in a prescribed line. Erratic movement, calculated to make the toy move in an upredicted direction, was introduced by a German, Hoffmann, in 1908. The element of unpredictability made these toys very popular with children, and between the wars German variations were widely known. Today, British manufacturers of clockwork toys include erratic-movement models in their catalogues. These combine the trip and balancing principles with the uncoiled spring action.

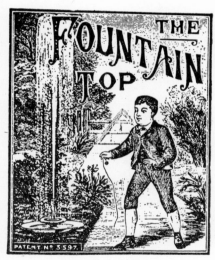

46. The Fountain Top   47. The Mikado

A striking example of American clockwork toy manufacture is the pair of dancing dolls in the Bethnal Green Collection. These are powered by a clockwork motor which agitates a rocker-bar on either end of which is a stout wire. The wires pass through small holes in the top of the box and project about four inches. The male and female negro figures sit loosely on the top of each wire and the jumping action of the rocker causes the puppets to jig. Loose wire connections

48. The Horse Race (gyro and flywheel)

49. The General

at the shoulders and thighs, together with jointed ankles, give free
and natural movements. The jigging dance will continue for twenty
to thirty minutes at one winding (51).

In the Equestrienne (45) the motive power is derived from the
spinning by a pulled string of a top or flywheel, supported in a
frame attached to the bar to which the horse is fixed. As the spindle
of the top spins on the bevel edge of the circular base, the horse
is caused to gallop round in a circle. And, being supported on the
table by a roller mounted eccentrically on its axis, it prances up

and down as it runs. The acrobat is attached to a light lever pivoted on the rotating frame and revolving with it. Twice in its revolution this lever is lifted by a cam forming part of the base. The first lift causes the figure to give a little bow. The second, which is much greater, makes her leap over the bar, while the horse runs under it.

A variation of the spinning action was used in a toy elephant. In this little machine the flywheel, with its vertical shaft, resembled an umbrella spread over the nabob who sat on top. The vertical shaft passed into the body of the elephant, and there, by a simple frictional gearing, rotated two cranks to which the legs were connected. The effect of spinning the umbrella was therefore merely to move the legs backwards and forwards. If that were all, however, no forward motion could be effected. But each foot of the nabob rested on a little wheel or roller, which could rotate only in one direction. In this way, while it caught the ground in its backward stroke, it rolled freely over it while moving forward, and so each leg in its turn contributed to the forward movement of the toy.

The French toy clockwork tricycle (71) has black cast-iron wheels, 4.8 inches and 4.3 inches in diameter, and a blue mechanism-cover. The boy riding is dressed in red coat, horizontally striped trousers and tall boots. He has pressed brass hands. Above the winder are the words 'PAT Feb 1st 187–Jan 22 187–'. The length is eleven inches and the height eight inches.

Another example of historical interest was in the form of two dancers, a military officer in uniform and his partner in a crinoline. Made of metal, the crinoline was grooved like a top, so that the string could be wound around the pear-shaped surface. String-propulsion gave the needed force and velocity to set the couple dancing and pirouetting on the table's surface.

These ingenious toys were short-lived because the golden era of clockwork came to supersede them, rather after the fashion that the automobile came to banish more leisurely and elegant conveyances.

The application of the sand-motor to toys occurred early in the nineteenth century, when French and German ingenuity outbid each other for the world market. The toys were constructed in wooden boxes, with cardboard figures framed in glass. The mechanism consisted of a system of wheels so interrelated that the sand, concentrated in the top of the cabinet, would trickle through apertures—on the hourglass pattern—and set into motion figures connected by wire or cord to the wheels and ratchets. These sand-toys are now very rare, but three are part of the Muir Collection. These contain cut-out figures which dramatically go through movements against a painted-in background. One is a street hurdy-gurdy player, surrounded by children; another a knife-grinder; and a third represents a group of cats dressed as acrobats in a circus tableau of trapeze and cycle acts.

Movement induced through the force of gravity led to the invention of many simple devices for imbuing toys with novelty and refinement. The German toy industry excelled at such improvements. The celebrated tumble-toys of the nineteenth century, utilising the counterpoise principle, were a French elaboration. One of the English penny-toys was the Flutter Toy, which dates from about 1820. A row of wooden beads, each with a feather stuck at one end to represent birds, are lifted to the top of a row of upright taut wires. As they shudder their way towards the base little by little, down the wire, they give an impression of fluttering.

Gordon Craig selected this design for the title page of his *Book of Penny Toys*. The Flutter Toy has recently reappeared in English shops newly and oddly rechristened "Wally, the Cheeky Woodpecker."

The rocker idea has its origin in the traditional cradle, *e.g.* the Moses basket, mounted on two segments of wood to create a rocking motion. Before the toy horse was mounted on rockers to give the illusion of a cantering action, it passed through its "prehistoric" and medieval phases.[1] From the simple horse of baked clay to the same model mounted on wheels represented thousands of years in mankind's mechanical skill. From the small horse-and-chariot pull-toy to the folk-toy of the Middle Ages (the ceremonial hobby-horse) represented another epochal advance. From the hobby-horse on wheels of the seventeenth century to the first English rocking-horse, which consisted of head, neck and saddle surmounted on its home-made boat-shaped rockers (56), the time-lag is much shorter. Then, as the rocking-horse became a toy which every father wished to give his small son, the design changed fundamentally. There began to appear more horse and less rocker. Soon, as craftsmen in wood took delight in fashioning toy horses having a closer fidelity to prancing palfreys and champing steeds, the legs were no longer clamped to the rockers but remained in a normal standing position, fixed to a wooden stand. This was then pegged to the rockers, and produced a more realistic horse. The next stage was when metal wheels were affixed

[1] Karl Gröber, *Children's Toys of Bygone Days*, Plate 140.

50. Novelty tableau toys from Central Europe, c. 1870. Performing bears revolve
by turning handle; donkeys bray if squeaker base is pressed

51. Dancing negroes: crank-operated American movement toy, c 1880

52. Clockwork merry-go-round, c. 1905, copied from one at Blackpool

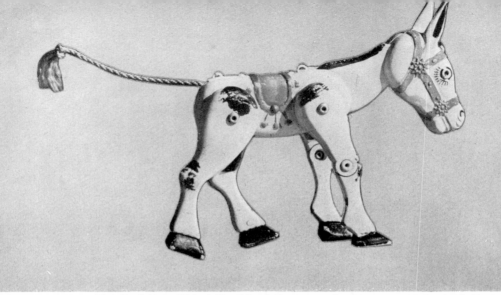

53. Toy Evolution: (*Below*) Traditional Burmese string puppet and (*above*) Muffin the Mule in cast metal, popularised by the Hogarth Puppets

to the board, transforming the horse at choice into a combination of the rocking animal and a wheel-toy.

These superb examples were covered in real cowhide. They were stitched by hand over a hand-carved frame, and were sold in English shops from 1800 onwards. In their workmanship they are unsurpassed and in their beauty of design can be distinguished easily from the German models in wood and plaster as depicted by Gröber.[1]

54. Child with hobby-horse and wind toys. *From a wood engraving by "Meister J.R.," c.* 1600.

Rocking-horses have been made in England for generations. It is a unique experience to discuss their finer points with such craftsmen as Herbert Staines, standing by his bench in the famous Lines Brothers factory in Morden. One is informed about the massive Number 7 model, which stood a good ten hands high before being mounted on its stand. Then one is introduced to the smaller carthorses ("white mice" used to be the craftsmen's term for them!); one is given technical enlightenment on the making of the hobby-horses, no longer

[1] Karl Gröber, *Children's Toys of Bygone Days*, Plates 249–251.

seen by the modern child. These apparently, were simply heads (carved in the same way as the heads of rocking-horses) mounted on a hobby-stick—after the Chinese pattern. These workers also turned out the colossal wooden models of horses made for saddlers' shops—those we used to see behind plate-glass windows, fully harnessed, a sign of times when horse-traffic was common. To handle the razor-sharp shaping-knife, the file rasp, the chopper and other tools by which the skill of a cunning carver can make a snorting steed's head out of a crude block, furnishes a link with a handicraft which now seems doomed to disappear (57).

55. Playing with a rocking-horse. *From an early nineteenth-century engraving*

The operation is slow and requires much patience. The head and body are carved from yellow pine and the legs from beech. After seasoning they are assembled, painted, and a mane and a tail from real cows' tails are affixed. The bodies are then harnessed and mounted on their stands by means of swing-irons, which Mr. Staines remembers as having been the method used for rocking since 1913.

Much has been written about rocking-horses, and both Gröber and Mrs. Jackson show illustrations of old models. An almost surgical description of this romantic—and still very-much-kicking—traditional toy is given by a writer who has made a comparison between design in everyday things of the nineteenth and twentieth centuries:

"Wooden horses are like Dutch dolls and are similarly distorted, but pleasant. The rocking-horse is a slightly more realistic animal, mounted on parallel bars that swing on steel rods in a frame: it is neither so exciting nor so dangerous as the nineteenth-century version, which really was on rockers and could be easily overturned, but the horse remains the same. It is made of wood or composition and painted dapple grey. The mane and tail are real horse-hair and a glass eye glares above the wooden teeth. Recently a dapple grey galloping horse made of pressed steel has been intro-

56. English rocking-horse with pillion seat and holster for pistols bearing traces of coloured design, from the seventeenth century

57. Hand-carved English horse mounted on swing-irons, *c.* 1920

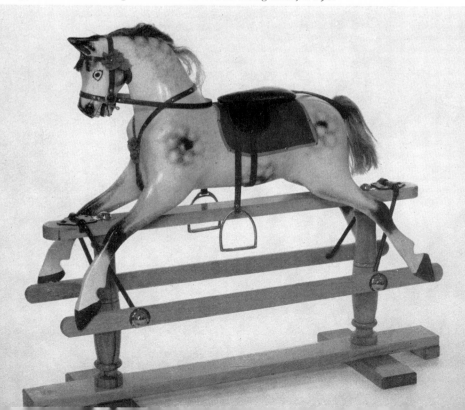

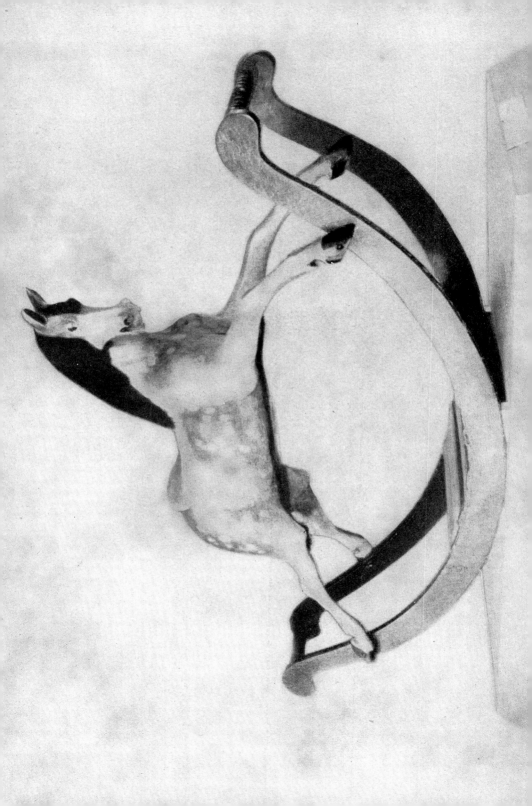

duced. It has lost all the sharp ferocity of the wooden horse and is coloured with a spray-gun."[1]

Wheels and leverage are methods of inducing movement in the toy which constitute in themselves a significant chapter in sociological research. It seems likely that the first wheels were in the form of rollers, that is, actual trunks of trees; and that later the trunk was sliced into sections with holes bored through them for the axles to run on. A study of the first wheels primitively carved out of wood, such, for example, as those on the toy horse at the British Museum dating from *c.* 500 B.C., show them to be devised in the same way and having similar axle-pins[2] to those on sixteenth-century wooden horses in the Nuremberg Museum.

When the first Egyptian used his first wheel for a child's toy a technical revolution had begun which in turn has influenced man's spiritual and cultural growth. This is evidenced by an examination of the wheel in industry, literature, art and all those forms in which man's creative spirit has been manifest, both for good and for evil.

The chariots of baked clay, drawn by horses or mules, which have been unearthed from the tombs of Greek children are equipped with wheels dating from 1200 B.C.

One of the most effective ways of making a child conscious of the processes in machinery, or mechanical apparatus of any kind, is by introducing them to wheel-toys at an early age. This educational approach, hitherto not attempted in England, has been successfully adumbrated by American teachers in the *Basic Studies in Science* series, teaching simple technical processes through play apparatus.[3]

The story of toy trains in all respects is analogous to that of the sailing-boat. They also travel in and out across the disputed frontier-line nebulously separating toys from models. It was not so very long after Stephenson that the first quantity-steam locomotive, built to scale proportions and to standard gauges defined that year, was produced. This sensational model was the work of Bassett-Lowke in the year 1901. It was an intermediate type between the earliest efforts then attempted and the *Lady of the Lake* express locomotive in gauge $1\frac{3}{4}$ inches, fitted with oscillating cylinder.

---

[1] Barbara Jones, *Unsophisticated Arts.*
[2] Horses mounted on wheels having either axle-pins or protruding hubs are at: Alexandria Museum (Egyptian, 500 B.C.); Spielzeug Museum, Sonneburg (Cypriot, 1000 B.C.); Munich Museum of Modern Art (Greek).
[3] *How Do We Know?* (Scott Foresman Company, New York).

58. Early nineteenth-century English horse-on-rockers

Such achievements as these were being perfected at the same time as the early toy locomotives which were made in France and Germany and utilised the flywheel drive for motive-power propelled by a piece of string (63).

It was not so very long until that other famous British maker of model railways, Frank Hornby, built up another world reputation for English mechanical inventiveness through his constructional toy Meccano.

59. Battery-driven model of a London tramcar, 1910

In a sense Frank Hornby's name should be added to the roll of the great toy-makers already mentioned. Not the least of his achievements was his success in welding together Meccano boys of all nationalities into the world-wide fellowship of the Meccano Guild. A few years later he founded the Hornby Railway Company, the purpose of which is to guide young railway enthusiasts along the right lines in developing their miniature railways, and thus enable them to obtain the greatest enjoyment from their hobby.

The inventor of these two very different forms, Hornby Trains and Meccano, commenced work in an office of a Liverpool firm of

60. Steam-driven model of the *Rocket*, 1901

importers, where he rose to be chief managing clerk. He never abandoned his mechanical pursuits, however, and as the years passed by
he gradually acquired a useful equipment of tools and a good all-
round knowledge of engineering principles and methods. As his two
sons grew up, he delighted in making toys for them, and encountered
difficulty in meeting their continual demands for new ones. He soon
found that new parts had to be made for every new toy, because
most of the parts used in his previous toys were useless for any but
their original purpose.

61. Railway Station Accessories, 1910
Left: Refreshment Waggon. *Right:* Porter's barrow

While casting about for some way of reducing waste of time and
material, he noticed a large crane in operation. As Hornby watched
it he was struck by the essential simplicity of its construction. The
idea occurred to him that a model of it could be built with a comparatively small number of easily made parts. Following up this idea,
he gradually thought out a scheme of perforated parts that could be
bolted together in any required positions and which could afterwards
be unbolted and reassembled in different arrangements.

Full of enthusiasm for his new idea, Frank Hornby bought a large
sheet of copper and a pair of shears, and hurried home to experiment
with a series of perforated strips. Mr. Roland G. Hornby, his elder
son, speaks of the excitement which prevailed on that evening, and
on many subsequent ones, as he helped his father to prepare the parts.

The strips were all cut to a width of half an inch, their lengths
being respectively two and a half inches, five and a half inches and
twelve and a half inches. These were perforated with equal-sized
holes at half-inch intervals, this being the special task assigned to
the son. The method by which he assembled components is of interest.

Suitable rods and bolts were obtained from a watchmaker. All-
though Frank Hornby spared no effort, he could not find nuts of the

correct size, so he was obliged to make these himself. Angle brackets for fastening the strips together at right angles were cut out of sheet copper. Wheels provided the next problem, for none of suitable size and construction could be bought. The inventor, accordingly, had to work out his own design and have the wheels cast for him in a local brass foundry and then turned on the lathe.

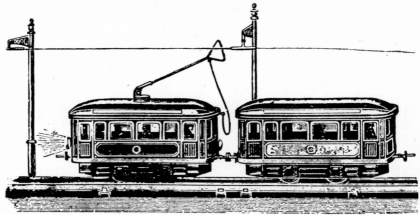

62. Continental-type electric tramcars, taking power from overhead cable, 1910

The next problem was to devise a suitable method of fixing the wheels on the rods. The usual collar and set-screw would, of course, have been satisfactory, but at the time this method seemed to him to be too expensive for his requirements, and he adopted a steel clip for the purpose. Subsequently he abandoned the clip in favour of the set-screw.

Long and weary hours passed before all the parts were ready for trying out, but he was encouraged by the growing certainty that he was working along the right lines. At last the great day came when he built up the first Meccano model. This was a crane which ran on wheels and luffed and jibbed in the same manner as a real one. It was with boundless pleasure that Hornby and his sons built that first crane, taking it to pieces and building it up again! Before they attached the jib, the base of the crane looked so much like a truck that they added a few more strips and made it into a real truck that could run on rails formed of strips. Then it was found that the parts could be used to construct a whole range of other models.

Next a patent agent was consulted and the necessary protection

63. Friction and flywheel-driven locomotive, French, *c.* 1860
64. Clockwork-driven London omnibus, rubber-tyred

65. Edwardian toy train; gaily painted carriages have sliding roofs
66. Early toy-steam engine, *c.* 1890—1900

for the great idea obtained. In January 1901 the English patent was granted, and foreign patents followed in due course.

Later, Frank Hornby often said that he wondered whether he would ever have tackled the task of developing his invention if he had foreseen the trouble and difficulties he was destined to encounter. At first matters seemed hopeless. He approached one firm after another with a view to their manufacturing and marketing the toy, but without success. He then had the happy idea of submitting photographs and details of the toy to Professor Hele-Shaw, who at that time was Professor of Engineering at the Walker Engineering Laboratories, University College, Liverpool. In his reply Hele-Shaw expressed the opinion that the scheme was based on sound engineering principles and that it should have great success as a constructional toy. This letter was of great aid to the inventor in enabling him to obtain the financial assistance necessary to have the parts manufactured for him.

The toy, to which he gave the name *Mechanics Made Easy*, was now actually in being, but troubles were not over.

It was about this time that the name *Mechanics Made Easy* was changed to the handier and shorter one of *Meccano*. The new name was registered in England on September 14, 1907. Ever since it has been the mark of the genuine Hornby system.

The same problem of "Toy-or-Model?", which we shall consider in relation to soldiers, arises again when we think about boats, locomotives, aircraft, vehicles. Modern tooling methods, particularly a switching-over from wood to plastic, permit of a sharper detail through mass-production. It is a fact nowadays that, as far as toy vehicles for boys are concerned, fidelity in the replica to the original, whether it be motor-launch, tractor, ambulance or crane, has become almost a necessity.

So remarkable in their scaling are some of these modern toys that it is difficult in certain instances to decide whether they are, in fact, "toys" or "models". One can safely leave such wrangles over definition to the pedants of Toymanship!

Toy boats, and sailing them, are an integral part of every child's experience; and to watch the fiercely burning devotion with which grown men assist at communal sailings on freezing-cold Sundays, be it in Kensington Gardens or on Hampstead Heath, makes one acutely aware of the characteristics of an island people. Despite this, however, there seems to be remarkably little pictorial record of the kinds of boats which boys played with down the ages. Supposedly, most of the better boats were lovingly carved out by old salts for their own satisfaction, and later fell into the expectant hands of youth. Many of these were of the model class, and in Mr. Bassett-Lowke's book on the subject[1] are found pleasing drawings in colour of (i) a fighting ship of Queen Elizabeth I's reign; (ii) the splendid *Cutty Sark* model at South Kensington Science Museum; (iii) the famous fourteen-feet-long scale-model H.M.S. *Hood*, which took twelve months to build and which was exhibited at the British Empire Exhibition at Glasgow in 1938; and (iv), last word in streamlined modernity, the largest model of the largest ship in the world, the R.M.S. *Queen Elizabeth.*

67. English steam-driven model fire-engine, 1910

A vivid reminiscence of an English lad's childhood is included by Cyril Beaumont in his book inspired by the kind of impromptu games which enriched the impressionable years of children blessed with imagination and eager to improvise in their play:[2]

"Down another flight and there was the bathroom, where I used to sit in the bath, which I filled almost to the brim, and swayed my body from side to side until the water took on a swell, and oft cascaded to the floor. In these home waters I floated

[1] Bassett-Lowke, *Models* (Puffin Books).
[2] C. Beaumont, *Flashback, Stories of My Youth*, p. 7.

68. Wooden toy train, German, *c.* 1845. Wheels fit into grooves of inclined track on adjustable supports

69. Double-purpose horse-on-wheels used as a pull-along which can also be clamped to rockers

70. First German toys exported after World War II. Turkey's tail and wings outspread; ball swivels for playing kitten

71. One of the earliest French clockwork toys, *c.* 1870 (see page 79)

my destroyer, the hulk of a one-time yacht, now painted black and provided with bulwarks fashioned of pins and thread, and a bridge and funnels contrived from a cigar-box and cocoa tins. Some veteran soldiers placed on the deck did their best to acquire sea-legs while the ship rocked and dipped in the stormy seas. Now and again there was a splash which told of a man overboard and then, almost immediately afterwards, came the silvery tinkle which announced that he had reached the cradle of the deep."

Early model craft made for children of ancient Egypt or China are not commonly seen in museum collections. The much-publicised models in the British Museum Egyptian Room, made of clay and terra-cotta, are really "Spirit Ships", designed entirely for a semi-religious purpose. Similarly, such gorgeous examples of oriental patience, art and accuracy as are found in the ivory model of a Chinese mandarin's houseboat point rather to adult play than to any fishpond in the royal palace.

My own schooldays were never glorified by possession of such miraculous sailing-boats as scale models. My schoolmates were content to sail a half-crown yacht in rock-pools, or to launch a crudely home-made galleon on the wild waters of "The Horse Pond"—a village crossroads where dairymen, returning from their city rounds, would stop to water their horses and to welcome the curious entertainment provided by our obsessions. Perhaps more memorable than anything else were those days of pelting rain which turned the roadside runnels into crashing, mud-brown torrents, and when, our lessons over, we lanched a thousand paper boats, or ruler-and-pencil flotillas, upon the sewer's flood.

As in other types of toy, social patterns and industrial change are reflected in the different ways in which craft *move* along the water's surface. The first, and one imagines the most popular, source of power is wind. The sail-in-the-wind should fill any healthy lad with a zeal for navigation, or the love of adventure. Millais expressed it in his painting, *The Boyhood of Raleigh*. Indeed, models of sailing-ships made by old salts were probably the first elaborate toys in this class.

There can be no doubt but that modern boys are entirely thrilled by such devices as wireless-control, a "mystery" system whereby Mr. Victor B. Harrison, well-known among model enthusiasts, can control the speed and the direction of his steam model of the *Mauretania*.

With the chronological disappearance of sailing ships, a new power came to drive the toy boat, the discovery of steam. The first type of steam-toy was fitted with a reciprocating engine, consisting of a boiler and a small cylinder. Next followed clockwork; and later came solid fuel. This last was a reaction-propulsion whereby a hot stream of air is driven into the water.

At about this time elastic was entering toy design in a new way. Its possibilities as a motive power had been recognised and toy boats were driven along by rubber, on the same principle as the contemporary toy aircraft, which was a technical innovation of some importance. Compressed air was the next stage. How well one remembers those lightly built wooden boats, and how incredibly long and thin they seemed to be! And, in the stern, that small three-cylinder radial motor driving a tiny screw.

Chemicals were not overlooked by the toy-boat builders. They actually applied the use of camphor. It seems a long time ago, but many will recall the celluloid bath-toys, small boats that moved mysteriously by the reaction of a camphor pellet fixed to the stern. This "magic" can be explained in layman's language as the chemical action of camphor on water which causes, as it were, a gentle pushing-forward of the craft.

Then came electricity. James Vanderbeek has told me he could remember the two small storage-cells; and the home-made electric motor (about twenty-four inches long); and the magnet made from one of the earliest radio loudspeakers; and the armature—a piece of cast-iron hacked out by hand—which his father, a radio expert, utilised in making for him "that *Mayflower* of all electrically driven toys." (We have moved forward so rapidly in scientific development that neatness and precision are features we take for granted. How neat, how precise, for instance, is the newest one-and-three-eights inch permanent-magnet motor, looking in its blue plastic casing like a small mustard cruet, yet turning at over six thousand revolutions a minute when driven off a simple flash-lamp battery!)

Before we reach the Internal Combustion Engine stage, a word should be said about Flash-steam. This is a form of steam-propulsion created by a boiler which works at a very high pressure, and of which the power output is twice as much as that in the original low-pressure engines already mentioned.

The combustion engine is now a recognised part of our daily lives, regarded no longer as being any more wonderful than the wheel, the sand or the spring which once, in the development of automatism, were scientific "bombshells."

We are familiar with petrol-driven boats; with boats driven by what you and I know as *Diesel,* but which engineers prefer to call

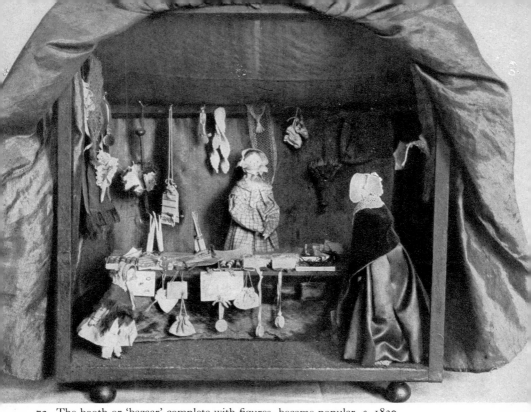

72. The booth or 'bazaar' complete with figures, became popular, c. 1830
73. English pedlar dolls, with leather faces and hands, c. 1780

Compression Ignition. Finally, there were manufactured toy boats driven by hot-coil, or glow-plug ignition.

Jets, we should be thankful, have not yet been introduced by the children into honest men's homes. Nevertheless, it is of interest to record that the Rocket principle is now applied in toys marketed by a firm manufacturing a range of boats, motors, aircraft, helicopters and similar mechanicals. This is another British invention which may rightly be said to have won the laurels for inventiveness and originality in toy-making, and which is, in a sense, in the direct tradition of Cox, Maillardet, Bassett-Lowke and Hornby.

74. Wooden play-doll, *c.* 1780, from the collection of Mrs. R. H. Hyde-Thompson

V

DOLLS AND DOLLS' HOUSES

THE word *doll* is a comparatively new arrival into the English vocabulary. One of the earliest references occurs in a 1751 edition of the *Gentleman's Magazine*, though it seems likely that *doll* was current usage in the speech of the early eighteenth century. Several theories exist as to its etymological origin, of which the most generally accepted, because most linguistically obvious, is that the word derives from the Greek εἰδωλον, the root-concept for *idol*. Another is that the word grew from the pet-name for Dorothy, which may have had some circumstantial connection with the change of terminology. Whether that variant replaced the Latin root *pupa* (English *puppet*, French *poupée*, German *puppe*) cannot be established for certain, but it is clear that the use of *doll* to express a toy is quite a modern development.

Dolls are not, as has been assumed all too readilly, age-old archetypal playthings, passing down with only superficial changes from pre-Christian civilisations in Mesopotamia and the Indus lands, and fulfilling fundamentally the same juvenile interests.

Nothing could be further from the facts. What are regarded unequivocally as dolls representing ancient cultures were simply objects of ritualistic and sacred import. They have absolutely no association with the toy idea. Students who have investigated these social systems have produced evidence for assumptions which have in turn been strengthened by such recent excavations from the Harappa civilisations at Mohunjodaro Chandarro, North-West India,[1] that the female effigies so often labelled in museum collections as "ancient toy" were, indisputably, objects of magico-religious significance. Sometimes they filled the role of talismans, tiny luck-symbols of a kind still found in some Arab countries. These are unique among Semitic peoples, whose outlook towards "graven images" has been largely conditioned by the Old Testament taboo on graphic or sculptural representation. That many Mohammedan countries have the cloth doll is attributed to the Islamic tradition that Ayesha, the child-bride of the Prophet, "brought her dolls to her new home." In India,

[1] Sir. J. Marshall, *Mohunjodaro and the Indus Civilisation*, 1931.

Turkey and Persia noble families keep as heirlooms dolls representing finely dressed women, some wearing the veil.

Sometimes these figures and figurines had specific godhead attributes. They were set up on shrines and altars for set religious purposes. Others were fetishes used in cult-worship. In Hindu belief, god-heroes are wrought to resemble doll-figures.[1] Several types were originally produced as phallic symbols, having the expressed idea of embodying practices associated with some primitive cult extolling procreation and the affirmation of eternal life. Identification with death-journeys and the progress of the spirit through regions in time and space were the tomb-figures called *Ushabti*, found in great numbers near the Egyptian grave-sites.

Much confusion in the public mind has been caused through tourists having bought these as "dolls" and so perpetuating this idea in all good faith. It is tempting, just because a figurine picked up in an Eastern or Asiatic bazaar resembles a play-piece of our century, to project on to it a similar role, and read into its *raison-d'être* pre-suppositions which are quite outside its scope or function.

In this category are many images, about six feet high, modelled in clay and covered with a dull turquoise glaze. They are often automatically designated as toys, but never were so in fact. The *Ushabti* and *Uashbiti* represented the Egyptian workers who were buried together with their master, and who would serve him in the after-life as they did in this life. They were known as "answerers" from their duty, which was to answer the call of their dead master or mistress. These replicas were made available in very large numbers. They were sold cheaply, so that even the very poor could purchase immunity from slavery after death. Buried together with the corpse, they were as inseparable from the interment as those symbols of kingly or spiritual election such as are placed in coffins during our own day. Child-slaves were also permitted to take these small answerers with them into the tomb. Consequently many of the child skeletons in excavated graves have been assumed to be those of children buried with their dolls, when no conception of a plaything was ever involved.[2]

Other interesting instances of such misrepresentation are the Egyptian "paddle-dolls" in the British Museum. These have on occasion been described (by Gröber among others)[3] as examples of

[1] A. Mookerjee, *Folk Art in Bengal.*

[2] A. P. Cole, *Notes on the Wenham Collection (U.S.A.) of Dolls and Figurines,* p. 18

[3] Karl Gröber, *Children's Toys of Bygone Days,* Plate XII.

toys. They have also been indentified with the faiences, and models of painted ships, soldiers, granaries, breweries and kitchens. They were actually funeral offerings, representing the vassals, armies and victuals on earth enjoyed by a king or grandee, which he would need to accompany him on his predestined way after death.

These paddle-dolls shaped from strips of flat wood, brightly painted and having tresses of hair made from strung dark beads, the famous Tiger Attacking a Man, and Tiger with Movable Jaws, are all in the British Museum collection.

Upon examining them closely, one always felt a sharp distinction between their crudely fashioned torsos, lacking both arms and legs, and the realistic figurines of carved and polished wood—replicas of the female body which exemplify a sophisticated sculptural sense and which are idols: carvings made to be worshipped. One was also puzzled at a contrast so obvious, and showing so little in common between the female votive objects and the paddle-dolls.

Such an intuition is confirmed by Petrie's excavations, which resulted in the discovery that these so-called "paddle-dolls" were really tomb-figures representing concubines, "without feet so that they would not run away."[1] The paddle-doll theory has been finally disproved by an essay in the *Brooklyn Museum Journal* by Mrs. E. Riefstahl.[2] Whereas the writer can find no evidence, either for or to the contrary, that little Egyptian girls did indulge in doll-play, and is noncommittal on this point, she declares that all the recent evidence is on the side of there not having been dolls. Her conclusion is that " . . . from the paddle-dolls of the Middle Kingdom down to the terra-cottas of Roman times, none of the female figurines found in Egypt were dolls—but primarily images with magical or religious properties." It is fortunate that the extraordinarily favourable climate of Egypt has kept these objects in such a good state of preservation.

The same is true of the marble figures from children's graves as drawn by Herčík. These are female effigies bound with ropes.[3] They may, possibly throughout a later era, continue the same idea of concubinage.

The finds from ancient Greece have an entirely different shape and are, for the most part, jointed. The jointed dolls are of burnt clay, with the limbs separately hooked on by string or cord features,

---

[1] *Objects of Daily Use*, p. 59.

[2] *Brooklyn Museum Journal*, 1943, p. 9.

[3] *Folktoys*, p. 48.

which so resemble the modern jointed doll that its evolution from these origins is unmistakable.

In considering the continuity of design, it becomes clear that during the past five thousand years, two basic patterns have been repeated and seldom diverted from. One is the representation of the figure made from a single lump, like a piece of broomstick or a clothes-peg, in which the head, costume and limbs are painted on the surface. The second is a more dynamic treatment. It shows head, neck, shoulders, arms, legs and facial expression as separate entities but shaped out of the single unit.

The former survives in the dolls of the poor child. It is common both to the one-piece dolly made from a meat-bone with pencilled-in eyes, nose and mouth, and dressed in rags (now in a museum, but fifty years ago played with in an East End slum) and to the penny dolls sold in the booths of India and Ceylon to this day. The latter are illustrated in the coloured frontispiece to Mookerjee's *Folk-Art in Bengal*.

The second treatment derives from the sophisticated Egyptian tomb-figures. Illustrations show them as having all the aesthetic elements of traditional European sculpture, which reached technical perfection in the mechanical dolls of the sixteenth century. It perpetuates a basic pattern in development; as heterogeneous as the wooden dolls or contemporary primitive tribes (*i.e.* the Iroba dolls of Central Africa) and the latest baby doll in plastic, endowed with crying, eye-closing, wetting and washability as its normal attributes.

Describing the making of traditional representational dolls from clay by Bengali women, A. Mookerjee observed that they first pinch the clay free from any other foreign element. "To mark the eyes, ornaments or the pointed breasts of the hand-made figures, pellets are stuck into the body. Sometimes either the apple of the eye or the ornament of the limbs are shown either by perforation or by grooves."

On the question of sex-distinction it is of interest to find that the general trend in Eastern peoples has been to fashion the lower portion as a solid mass and that they do not indicate any mark of sex. Exceptions are the Alhadi dolls of Bengal, in which the makers continue to emphasise strong primary sexual characteristics.[1]

Japanese dolls, like other folk-toys of that country, derive from aspects of ancestor worship. They are deeply rooted in social custom

[1] A. Mookerjee, *Folk-Art in Bengal*, p. 12.

with which the cult-figures were associated.[1] When certain customs fell into disuse and were replaced by other forms the objects, placed with reverence over a shrine or in a place sacred to the memory of a family-member, were given to children and so, by a natural process, became playthings.

In Japan on March 3 of every year is held a doll festival for girls, called Hina Matsuri; while on May 5 festivals of warrior dolls are held for boys. Into these go the highest artistic standards of the nation, and the costumes and finish are the pride of those who have created them.[2]

Valuable information on this aspect of Japanese art is contained in a beautifully illustrated brochure by Tekiho Nashizawa, one of a series issued by the Japanese Travel Bureau of Tokyo in 1939.[3] In an endeavour to obtain reproductions of some of the drawings, which give a clearer impression than could any verbal description of their conception and colouring, I received a cordial letter from the Bureau's manager pointing out that the blocks were out of print. With unconscious humour, it was suggested that if I agreed to bear the expenses for the publication of a series of new blocks, "we would be pleased to submit to you an estimate at an early date."

From the pagan fetish to the doll used for semi-religious purposes is but a short evolutionary step. Like many customs taken over by the early Church and woven into the fabric of the Roman Catholic ritual, dolls were used to enact Mystery Plays. Arranged before the High Altar, and to commemorate the Nativity, the dramatisation of the scene in the Manger has been a common practice in Catholic churches. To the present day some churches are renowned for the naturalistic presentation of the Crib, where the Infant Jesus, portrayed by a doll, draws pilgrims from outside the parish.

Crèche-dolls as a means of commemoration at Christmas may have been begun in the thirteenth century by St. Francis of Assisi, for there is a record of such a Nativity tableau having been put on at an Italian church in 1223.[4]

Every conceivable suitable material has gone into the making of dolls. Such variety provides an index to the period and culture from which the design emanates. Wood, from prehistoric times, has

---

[1] Tekiho Nashizawa, *Japanese Folktoys*, p. 36.

[2] Lewis Bush, *Japanalia*.

[3] *Japanese Folktoys*.

[4] Freeman, *Cavalcade of Toys*, p. 44.

remained the staple raw material; terra-cotta, another ancient substance, is now confined to the making of ornamental toys. Other materials, which seem at the time of their general use to have the hallmark of permanence, are soon replaced by newer and more up-to-date stuff, which, in turn, enjoys an ephemeral popularity.

Dolls from hemp, flax and straw were made in the homes of farming communities long before the conventional materials reached the hamlets and villages. A crude example of a talisman in the form of a piece of braided flax, hung on the spinning-wheel and brought out to America by one of the early settlers, is part of the Wenham Doll Collection in the United States.[1] A link with harvest festivities preserved the ancient fertility customs discussed by Sir James Frazer,[2] and takes the form of traditional straw decorations made from a long twist of barley called a "neck." These are still found in parts of rural Essex, Devon and the West Country. They are sometimes called corn-dollies or, alternatively, kern-maidens.[3]

The centre of the English straw and marquetry industry was for many years at Luton. Here straw-plaiting, generally directed to the making of hats and baskets, was occasionally diverted by the apprentices to the turning-out of dolls. Two examples of these, dressed entirely in plaited straw, are at the Luton Museum. They carry small straw baskets filled with straw flowers. It is probable that they were designed as an early form of craft-advertisement, publicising the unique skill of the Luton workers.

In colonial America children played with dolls made from the husks of sweet corn. The husks were folded over the cob and tied across to make the head. The eyes, nose and mouth were painted with natural dyes on the dried surface, and the tassel-like corn-silk was the obvious substance for making the hair. These are not longer widely found, but it is thought that the pioneering children of America learned the art of making corn-husk dolls from the Red Indians.[4]

Another old-fashioned custom was the improvising of dolls from a towel, a table-napkin, or a large kerchief. The action of folding, rolling and the making of a knot for a head has given real pleasure to many a child and has produced an object on which to lavish affection. A ribbon pinned to the finished article lent an added attraction.

[1] *Notes on Wenham Museum Collection*, p. 34.
[2] *The Golden Bough.*
[3] M. Lambert and E. Marx, *English Popular Art*, p. 87.
[4] W. H. Chandlee, *Uncle Sam's Toys* (St. Nicholas Magazine, 1901, pp. 150–155).

In Henry Mayhew's masterpiece, *London Labour and the London Poor* (1851), his vivid studies of Cockney types, costermongers, street-traders, pedlars and itinerants of all kinds, includes a description of the hard life of the street-sellers of dolls, and of dolls' heads drawn from Houndsditch and Leadenhall Street.

Fashion-dolls, as Gröber points out, were devised by Parisian costumiers as early as the fourteenth century. It is on record that the Queen of England in 1391 had dolls sent to her which would demonstrate the modes then current at the French Court. When the dolls had served their purpose they were handed over to the small daughters of the palaces and mansions, where they were treasured as toys. Gröber's account also mentions that Anne of Brittany prepared a large doll as a present for Queen Isabella of Spain in 1497. Upon inspecting the gift she decided that it was not richly enough dressed and so gave orders for it to be entirely re-fitted out.

These fashion-dolls continued to be made in the nineteenth century until the French began to publicise their fashions in book and album form. These, produced in colour and of a high artistic standard, finally did away with the need for the dolls as ambassadors of the latest vogues.

As fashion-dolls began to disappear there arose a wide interest in the English Pedlar Dolls. These were all faithful replicas of street-traders and hawkers who were a common sight in the London of the late eighteenth century. Historians have speculated as to their function, but it seems certain, in view of the careful array of tiny wares laid out on their trays or in their baskets, that they filled a need to display the accumulating collections of knick-knacks which were at that time sold in the toyshops (73). Numerous miniature copies of articles of haberdashery (72), hardware, household utensils and food-stuffs were at that time sold for Baby Houses, and grown-ups, particularly teachers or governesses, devised the pedlar doll as a means of preserving the miniature objects in an appropriate setting. It is noteworthy that so many of these dolls have the faces of old women, and it is exceptional to come across men pedlars or dolls having the features of younger females. The accuracy of their dress, aprons, shawls, capes and bonnets, representative in every detail of the working-class clothes of the time, compares favourably with the splendour and grandeur of the costumes with which the first children's wax dolls were clothed.

In certain countries dolls made from cloth usually portray a special

75. English wax doll, *c.* 1820. Height 21 in.

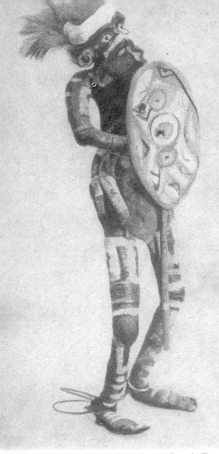

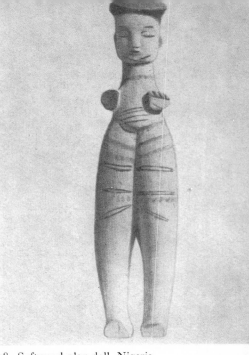

78. Softwood play-doll, Nigeria
79. Afrikaan missioner and wife, Bantu

76. Painted warrior, South Pacific
77. Wooden figurine, central Africa

regional trait or style. In Russia, Poland and America some splendid work was once done by expert needleworkers. In England stockings were sometimes used as the body, and were stuffed with shavings, cottonwool, sawdust or soft rags. Wool, and frequently real hair, was sewn into the cloth head. The features were either drawn in by pencil and painted over, or done with coloured inks. The limbs, without fingers or toes, were sewn on as separate parts. Early Rag-dolls were dressed in bright, flowered, full skirts. One variety was devised with two heads, a black and a white, which were interchangeable by covering up one with the teacosy-shaped skirt.

Though they were seldom beautiful, the rag-dolls were treasured for their softness and cuddly quality, and had the advantage of standing up to the trials of buffetings and caresses alike.

More sophisticated dolls made from cloth were the work of aristocratic ladies driven into political exile who were obliged to put their talents for needlework to commercial use. Their dresses were embroidered with meticulous care. So outstanding were they that they fetched high prices in the more exclusive shops.

During the nineteenth century it was Germany, as the great doll-producing country of Europe, which adopted different materials as they passed manufacturing tests. The first was wax; then came papier-mâché; later china, and then bisque. Most of these vanished from the mass-production market after the 1914-1918 war, when a series of new materials followed each other in doll manufacture. These included knitting-wool, celluloid, leather, washable italian-cloth, solid rubber, and light metals like tin or aluminium.

The most recent development is the use of soft rubber, with adjustable limbs which can be taken off for bathing, and various kinds of plastic materials.

A review of the different types will serve to show what an amount of experience and thought has gone into the making of dolls, of which more are sold in England every year than of any other toy.

Prints and portraits of the fourteenth and fifteenth centuries, in which children are shown playing with dolls, give evidence that the toys were then made of wood.

Wood, indeed, remained for several centuries the staple material from which dolls were made. The earliest examples are not stereotyped but are expressions of individual artists who, as a labour of love, fashioned and carved their figures in a very personal style. The first Wooden Dolls made to a pattern, and which became the common

6-79. Examples of primitive doll-making.

toy for about two hundred years in Europe, came from the Thuringian forest in Germany. There, where an abundance of wood existed, the peasants would spend their long winters producing crude little figures, admirably suited to dressing and play. They were boxed and collected by travelling merchants who included them among their wares and soon built up a wide demand in other countries for the wooden doll. In America they were called "Peg-dolls," and in some places "Pennywoods." In England they assumed the name of Dutch Dolls, because at one time England imported toys on a large scale from the Netherlands. Many of the examples of dolls' house furniture in museums were simply travellers' scale samples of household furniture which the Dutch salesmen would take with them to give potential customers an idea of what the finished article looked like. Among the toys imported in large numbers were dolls known as Flanders Babies—and later by the popular name of Dutch Dolls.

A fine example of an early eighteenth-century wooden doll is in the Victoria and Albert Museum. It has jointed limbs, delicately carved fingers and a head and body of painted wood. It is two feet four and a half inches in height, having a shoulder-width of four inches.

There are two fine examples of elegant English painted wooden dolls in the same collection. One is dressed in the costume of 1690 and sits in a chair of carved walnut. The doll is one foot nine inches high and has a shoulder-width of nine and a half inches. The second is dressed more ordinarily with flowered skirt, laced bodice and cape. It dates from the early 1700's, has jointed limbs, is two feet four and a half inches high and four inches across the shoulders.

The double-jointed wooden doll lent by Mrs. A. M. Moult to the 1851 Room at the Victoria and Albert Museum belonged to her grandmother. Describing it as "the smallest double-jointed doll in the world," its owner recounts that her mother and aunts, when small children, came across this treasure, which was completely dressed. Urged by childish curiosity, they "immediately denuded it and were severely reprimanded." The 1951 Exhibition was the first occasion on which this unusual doll was shown (84).

A penny-wooden, brought to America a century ago from Ireland, and now in the Wenham Collection, was called "grandmother's doll." Its battered body tells of years of hard play. The face, which is painted directly on the wood, lacks the white background on which the features were painted in German dolls, and it is an excellent example of a crude, home-whittled doll made in a peasant country.

These wooden dolls from the Continent enjoyed a long vogue. They were succeeded by the use of wax.

Working in wax was introduced into the fine arts about the fourth century. Artists found that making portraits in this medium was a lucrative profession. Soon the fashion grew of having wax models as memorials to departed friends. These were placed upon the walls of churches. By about the fourteenth century the walls had become so covered with commemorative models that they had to be removed from many churches for safety. These removals, coupled with the Reformation, which made a clean sweep of all images, reduced the scope for working in wax. Most of the portraits were destroyed, but a few were saved and cherished as religious objects; others were given to children as toys.

In Europe only royal sponsors could afford to commission funeral images of wax. The majority had to be content with miniature reproductions. The same skill which produced them moulded wax heads for fashion designers in France during the eighteenth century. They were elaborately dressed with wonderful hair-styles created for them, and imported to other European countries and to America as fashion-dolls. It is of interest that during the 1812 war so highly were these fashion-dolls valued that safe convoy was guaranteed to ships transporting them. Thus apart from the making of life-size figures for wax-works such as Madame Tussaud's, the wax-worker's talents turned to making play-dolls to meet the rising demand. The first heads were formed from poured wax made on a mould. They had painted hair and glass eyes. Because of the process, this solid-poured wax head has a certain monotony, yet with the individual dressing and attention which invests a toy with something of the owner's personality, the examples which have survived, somehow, look very different. Mrs. Jackson gives an illustration of such a head dating from 1810. Many of the heads were bought and affixed to a cloth body with limbs made of papier-mâché.

In the very early wax dolls, the cheeks and lips were painted directly on the wax surface; so too were the eyebrows and lashes.

Individuality was given to each face by the Montanari family, a leading firm who took up this trade in England. The Montanaris developed a method of embedding hair, strand by strand, into the wax with a hot needle. Their dolls became exceedingly popular and by the end of the eighteenth century the possession of a lovely wax doll was the height of the English girl's ambition. As the market grew, designs became competitive, and wax dolls were brought within the price range of ordinary folk.

The next technical advance, and one which was pioneered in England (later to be imitated in Germany), was to make the doll-heads out of composition and coat them over with a thin layer of wax after the red cheeks, lips and eyelashes had been painted on the pink composition head (frontispiece).

Then glass eyes were introduced, but the exact date of the first glass eye cannot be established. There is said to be a wax doll dated 1750 with eyes of Stiegel glass made by Stiegel himself.

Some of these became the first sleeping dolls, when glass eyes were made to open and shut by a control-wire passing through the body and protruding from the side. Not till much later did the counter-balance shutting eyes arrive, worked by a system of lead weights.

In the early English wax dolls blue eyes were more common than brown, as they became fashionable when the young Queen Victoria came to the throne.

The wax doll remained the prize possession among a girl's toys until it was challenged by the doll made from bisque. During the 1914–1918 war no wax dolls were made.

Bisque was perfected at doll factories both in Germany and France. The French specialised in a very fine quality bisque. Finish and workmanship at the Jumeau factories gained for these dolls a world-wide reputation through their purchase by tourists making the "grand tour" during the 'eighties and 'nineties. The initiative was later snatched by the Germans and Japanese, who copied the French styles and used cheap labour and rationalised processes, until finally the Jumeau factory was driven out of business by their cheaper output.

A typical French bisque doll had a pinkish cast, a head with a swivel neck, pierced ears to take ear-rings, and stationary glass eyes. Sometimes the right and left hands, made by different craftsmen, showed distinctive modelling. Those made by the Jumeau works were usually accompanied by a doll's trunk which was artistically equipped with four costumes in fullest detail, a hoop-skirt, accessories and small jewellery.

A similar material, but of coarser texture, was called stone bisque. Heads made from this were a duller white with painted cheeks. It was of a cheaper grade used in the small jointed china dolls about three inches long.

Parian, by contrast, was a very fine material, lustrous, and resembling at times clear marble. The eyes were painted and the hair moulded.

When the secret was first discovered of kaolin, the ingredient which alone could produce the hard paste from which porcelain is made, it was jealously guarded throughout Germany. From such factories as Meissen great numbers of doll-figures were sent around the world, for Saxony was the leading supply source. Dolls' heads were made at one works where they enjoyed unrivalled monopoly. They were all of a pattern and imported by Austria, Switzerland, France, Italy, America and England, each of which superimposed on stereotyped heads the dress and characteristics of their national traditions. The industry brought huge profits, since the mortality of the china head was high and thus insured constancy of demand. A later feature of the industry, at a point when glazed china was giving way to unglazed bisque, was the appearance of penny china dolls, from about half an inch to three inches in length, all made in one piece, hollow and very popular while their novelty lasted.

As a natural reaction from porcelain, bisque and china dolls, there came a wave of "unbreakables." This was begun by the application of soft rubber, which offered wide scope, especially for the Baby Doll, which, at the beginning of the twentieth century, with its changed ideas about child development, was considered more suitable from a psychological viewpoint than was the elaborately and fastidiously dressed grown-up doll. In the nineteen-twenties, artists in Europe and America were designing baby dolls from infant models. Resemblance to the newly born child was the chief aim, and the use of rubber encouraged bathing in water. The latest advance into naturalism has been the production of a wetting doll which will drink from a bottle and is equipped with diapers.

Celluloid, another material adapted to moulding, was used for baby dolls because it was sanitary and washable. Originally an English invention, it was left to an American, Hyatt, to make it into a commercial proposition for toy manufacture. The process was imitated in Germany, Poland and Japan, and celluloid dolls of various qualities and sizes began to flood the markets. They were very inexpensive, and therefore were collected by children in large numbers. One of the familiar varieties was the well-known Kewpie range, of which the characteristics were a long upper lip, a cheery smile, retroussé nose and hanging kiss-curl. A wide-eyed, sidelong glance gave to it a mischievous expression. It was manufactured also in black celluloid as a piccaninny doll.

Parents often wonder why it is that their small daughters grow attached to dolls with black faces. Some psychologists might answer that the child is identifying the blackness of her darling with naughtiness. Thus, it is in the role of scapegoat and sweetheart in turn that the black doll is treated.

One of the reasons why the rise of celluloid dolls was short-lived was the inflammability of that substance. After some unfortunate accidents through fire, public attention was focused on safer materials, and the wooden and soft dolls came into their own again.

The tendency to use waste in the school handicrafts lesson and a growing interest among educationalists to utilise paper for toy-making have led to original three-dimensional dolls, all of paper. The framework for these has been plastic wire or pipe-cleaners, and strip-paper wound ribbon-wise around this base has given an effect reminiscent of the true folk-toy. Clothes made from cut crêpe-paper, buttons, belt and accessories cut out of stiff brown paper, and impressionistic features gummed on to the face from coloured, shiny clippings, add something of caricature and the sly humour which is typical of the newest dolls of the present age.

Peculiar to our present century has been the series of mascot-dolls which appear on the market in the shape of people, animals or whimsical creations from nursery-tales. These, popularised by all the weight of commercial publicity, enjoy a phenomenal success for a limited period before descending like a falling star into obscurity and nonentity as a newer star rises in the toy firmament and eclipses their memory. Most of these are soft toys or cuddlies, calculated to rival the doll in the small child's affection, and at times successful in ousting it entirely. One of these was the nursery character of Humpty-Dumpty—a satisfactory replica of the Sir John Tenniel illustration to *Through the Looking Glass*. Other doll-types inspired by children's stories have been A. A. Milne's *Winnie the Pooh* characters, and Alison Uttley's *Grey Rabbit* series. Mabel Lucie Attwell dolls, with flesh-coloured velvety legs and arms, and dressed faithfully after the Attwell studies, enjoyed a meteoric vogue.

The creation of the *Crazy Cat* strip cartoons in American papers led an Australian cartoonist, Pat O'Sullivan, to invent an even more popular cat which he called Felix. This became a feature of a Pathé animated film called *Eve's Film Review*, introduced about 1922. Within a year and a half Felix had won a very wide popularity and his stuffed effigy became the hallmark of the happy playroom. In the same tradition have been Disney's Mickey Mouse, forerunner of a cavalcade of modern soft-toys, including Donald Duck, Pop-Eye, Snow White and Pinocchio.

Long before these American conceptions captured the interest of the young, certain fauna were regarded as indispensable Christmas gifts or birthday presents for children not already possessing them. They included Teddy Tail, the renowned *Daily Mail* mouse, whose adventures in that newspaper's comic strip for children first became a household word in the nineteen-twenties. A serious rival for English children's loyalty were two droll penguins and a long-eared bunny rabbit, sponsored by the *Daily Mirror*, known respectively as Pip, Squeak and Wilfred.

There were also two dog personalities whose names adorn the memorial plaque. One was Caesar, modelled from a photograph of Edward VII's pet, and made into a toy after the king's death in 1910. A label was tied around his neck bearing the legend: "I am Caesar, I belong to the King." Caesar had walked in the royal funeral procession and was the object of strong public sentiment.

Another dog favourite was Bonzo, a ridiculous mixture of bull-terrier, bulldog and smooth-haired terrier. The creation of an artist named Studdy, in his creator's words he was "a good caricature of his caricature of a dog." He was first launched by an English newspaper and christened "Bonzo" by the editor. The name stuck, and within eight years hundreds of thousands of children were familiar with this absurdly grinning creature and wore badges to his honour.

Yet another stuffed dog which has been described as an epic event in the English toy trade was a production of the Deans Rag Book Company in 1926. He was called Dismal Desmond, and responded to something in the mass-psychology which made him widely popular.

Other animals in this category were zoo favourites. First there were Jubilee and Booboo, mother and baby chimpanzees, dating from February 15, 1936; secondly, Barbara, the cubby bear; next, the Giant Panda; and more recently, Brumas, the white polar-bear cub.

The best-known equine type was Dobbin the carthorse, made by a London firm. He had a mass-following approaching that now enjoyed by Muffin the Mule, one of Annette Mills' television puppets.

Whereas these mascot-animals and animal-dolls come and go, two veterans of the toy kingdom seem to outlive and outlast their more casual companions. These are, first, the Golliwog, and secondly, the Teddy Bear.

The Golliwog is the English creation of a writer of children's books, Miss Upton. She derived the idea for this grotesque doll-personality from some old dolls which had been put away by her grandmother for many years. The result was *The Adventures of Two Dutch Dolls and a Golliwog,* which first appeared in 1895. A series of other doll books followed, telling about the adventures of Peg, Meg, Sarah Jane and The Midget. After the success of these characters, a children's card game was issued in which the Golliwog figured prominently.

The doll with a fuzzy-wuzzy head has its precedent in ancient times. Gröber gives a coloured photograph of the Coptic woven doll from Akhim Panapolis, dating from A.D. 500, now at the Sammlung Figdor in Vienna.[1] Its curious appearance and great shock of upstanding hair are as close a resemblance to the golliwog doll as has yet been found.

The Brown Bear had for centuries been a traditional toy among the children of Russia. The history of Russian folk-toys shows the symbolism to be as deeply rooted in the consciousness of that nation as, say, the emblematical associations of the Bulldog in Britain. Peasant-and-Bear wooden toys, of many varieties, dramatise the struggle between the land-workers and the primitive forces of nature. Russian nursery-lore is full of fables and anecdotes about Mishka the Bear.[2] It is noteworthy that during the nineteenth century English children knew the cubby-bear as Bruin, and that was the generally recognised name, like Bunny for rabbit, Dobbin for horse or Pussy for cat. Yet from about 1903 onwards the word Bruin disappears from the nursery vocabulary and the word Teddy takes its place. The reason lies in the fact that this was the year when a new toy, designed primarily as a boys' doll, broke all sales' records at the Leipzig Toy Fair. It was called Teddy's Bear, and was the result of a pooling of ideas by an American buyer from New York and a German designer named Frau Margarette Steiff of Württemberg.

The story goes that the buyer was visiting Frau Steiff's doll and soft toy factory in the Black Forest. While discussing the latest news,

---

[1] Karl Gröber, *Children's Toys of Bygone Days,* Plate I.

[2] J. Harrison and H. Mirrelees, *The Book of the Bear* (Nonesuch Press, 1926).

the American opened a Washington newspaper which had just published a cartoon showing Teddy Roosevelt after a bear hunt in the
Rocky Mountains. At his feet was a small bear which he had shot.
The trader, having an eye on the market, suggested that Frau Steiff
might make a doll in brown plush and, instead of a doll's head,
substitute a bear's. This, he argued, could be sold as a toy for small
boys. The idea appealed to her. Richard Steiff, her nephew, went to
the Zoological Gardens at Stuttgart and watched the comical antics
of the bear-cubs there.

Resulting from his observations, from her skill as designer and
manufacturer and from American stimulus, the first Teddy's Bear
appeared. During the subsequent year twelve thousand of these were
exported, mostly to America and England. By the year 1907 there
were four hundred factory hands and eighteen hundred women
working at home—all employed by the Steiff concern making these
toys. In 1908 the "growler" was introduced, which caused the toy,
when tilted backwards, to make an animal noise similar to the effect
of the squeaker apparatus in the crying baby doll. The next stage
was a dressed-up bear. Finally came the Teddy Bear Baby.

While this toy drama was unfolding in the Black Forest, the idea
occurred to British makers that, since the plush used in the German
bears came from Yorkshire, it would be feasible to manufacture
Teddies in Britain. In order to compete with cheap labour abroad, the
shape was modified. The long, thin Teddy was being made on the
principle of the German soft dolls of the period, which consisted of
a large bag for the body and four long thin sacks for each limb. The
English makers radically changed this shape by shortening the body,
making the limbs better proportioned and giving a plumper appearance to the animal. The earliest English bears were filled with kapok,
a soft, resilient, natural material grown mostly in Indonesia. The
head was enlarged and filled with wood-wool, a type of wood shaving
of a finer quality than that used for packing wooden cases. A new
method was perfected for joining the limbs which insured a tight fit
to the body. All wires that might injure a young child were left out.
This method of fixing is a closely guarded secret among the manufacturers of Teddy Bears to this day.

Toys in which growlers are inserted must be hand-filled with
wood-wool, as kapok, being soft and fluffy, would enter the holes of
the voice-box and prevent the growl from functioning.

In any discussion on toy design there is invariably a contrast made between the finer workmanship of long ago and the characterless mass-produced articles of modern times. From the aesthetic view-point the problem bristles with controversial issues, but none which raises such strong feelings as doll-design.

Commenting on this subject, a writer has stated forcefully that the average visitor to toy departments of large stores is depressed by the vulgarity of many stuffed animals and dolls.

"Among rolling eyes and leering expressions, grotesque but never humorous shapes, we often search in vain for a toy fit for the fresh imagination of the child who is to receive it. This has hardly been appreciated sufficiently by manufacturers. How many of the so-called soft dolls are really soft, especially when judged by our present-day standards of comfort ? The need for something to cuddle is such a natural instinct of childhood that it is surprising that more use has not been made of it. Here, for once, a little more realism in imitating the comfortable furry softness of animals would be more likely to meet with applause from the nursery than the tremendous efforts that are made at realism of appearance. The instinct of the child to imitate its parents has brought a crop of toys to satisfy it."[1]

When confronted with this argument, an English doll-salesman, having wide experience of the home and Continental trade for the past half-century, replied:

"It is a curious thing that nobody thought that dolls' faces were ugly thirty years ago. Yet these were all mass-produced by the same German firm and all of us English manufacturers were obliged to buy them from that source. The whole secret of combating mediocrity in a face is in the dressing . . ."

Thus, the debate continues. And, as a background to changing tastes, the magnetic attraction exerted by dolls, on children and adults alike, does not grow less as our cultural trends move away from the innocent and the unsophisticated. Such perpetuation of a deep human obsession lies thinly covered in most of us. It may be awakened by the sight of a well-rubbed fetish once fingered by witch-doctors; or the ancestral effigies used in the Roman villas as household gods. It may be excited by the gay dolls of clay found in the tombs of the Incas of Peru, or by the paper dolls made in China to represent members of the family. Racial memory may be kindled in all of us through the eating of a doll made from jelly, resuscitating an awareness of dolls made from bread which were eaten in the Middle Ages; while the munching of a Gingerbread Man in the family circle possibly revives, in some mysterious way, the consciousness of those who used to eat dolls made of sugar or chocolate in the days of Leonardo da Vinci.

[1] What a Doll Ought to Be, *Design for Today*, December 1933.

80. Play-doll, *c.* 1820, of articulated wood with face moulded of plaster-of-Paris on wooden base

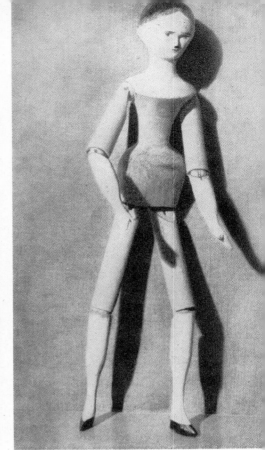

81. Wax character doll from *School For Scandal*
82. French fashion-doll, Jumeau factory, *c.* 1870

83. Articulated 'Dutch' doll (Thuringian)
84. Jointed baby doll, *c.* 1851

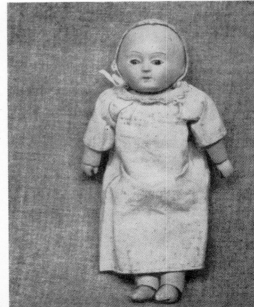

Handling of so many materials—beads, bone, amber, ivory, shell —suggests an extraordinary universality in the making of dolls down the centuries, so that the hobby of collecting any one of them, whether flax or wax or leather, iron or stone, wood or clay or cloth, once indulged, may lead to a delightful monomania.

"Sometimes they are a reflection of child psychology, sometimes they are a reflection of the economic conditions of a period. Occasionally they illustrate valuable benefit assets: alternatively they preserve in miniature customs and costumes long since forgotten."[1]

Both Gröber and Mrs. Jackson have concluded that doll-play, as a specific form of amusement for girls, goes back to the oldest of civilisations. It was not, however, until the mid-eighteenth century that a methodology of organised doll-play was fully worked out. This was inspired largely by the Germans, whose didacticism in the sphere of play led to the compiling of many charming, if more than thorough, books for the well-behaved junior fräulein. The influence came to England and stuck fast. Miss Alice Landells in her introduction to *The Girl's Own Toy-Maker and Book of Recreation* (1860) counselled: "My earnest desire has been practical in all respects, that this little book might become the medium of instilling into the young, habits which will lay the foundation of usefulness in after life." Her attitude, briefly, was that:

"Most mothers know the anxiety and trouble there is to keep children out of mischief and direct their young minds in the right way. For this purpose toys have long been resorted to as an innocent amusement, but these sometimes fail in their purpose, or get soon broken or destroyed, as their value is either not understood or properly felt, and a habit of destructiveness carelessly engendered which may ultimately have a pernicious effect on the future character of the child. But when taught to construct toys for itself, they are more likely to be valued, and the habit of preserving them ought to be carefully encouraged and promoted."

Dolls' Houses also were first elaborated in Germany. The finest craftsmanship went into their construction, and from the year 1700 onwards scale models were true works of art rather than toys for the amusement of children. They were kept in drawing-rooms and in special cabinets for the admiration of guests. Remarkably few of the early models have survived. These are now mostly in museums or in private collections. Examples of German, Italian and English houses may be seen at Bethnal Green Museum, but a more representative group may be found in the Victoria and Albert Museum.

[1] *Notes on Wenham Museum Collection.*

The early German examples include a four-room symmetrical two-storey house dated 1673. It is three feet six inches in height, three feet in width and one and a half feet in depth. The furnishings of the rooms, particularly the kitchen, are magnificent reproductions of the prevalent styles from Nuremberg of that period.

The English houses date from the early eighteenth century, when Queen Anne set a vogue in this direction. Both exterior and interior are of a quality equalling the Nuremberg houses, and the front façade of the 1760 model is complete with balustrades and staircase leading to the central balcony (86). Ornamental urns surmount a house dated 1740, which is copied from a three-storey mansion having fourteen front windows and a hall door with fanlight but without stucco pillars.

Until about 1850 the name Dolls' House was not used in England. The current term was Baby House, dictionaries defining a doll as "a child's baby" or "a girl's toy baby." A reference to the interest which these houses occasioned then occurs in a letter which Horace Walpole wrote to his friend Mann in 1750. "The Prince is building baby houses at Kew," he remarked. The allusion was to Frederick, Prince of Wales, who died the following year. During a visit to the Duke of Brunswick he had become fascinated by the task which the dowager duchess Princess Auguste Dorothea had set herself during a long widowhood. This was an ambitious plan to represent the entire Brunswick Court in miniature, and the German craftsmen were working hard to carry out her orders. The young prince formed a liking for the hobby and brought the interest back to London.

One of the finest examples of these houses specifically designed to amuse children is the Westbrook Baby House, dating from 1705. In that year a property owner left his residence in the Isle of Dogs, and as a mark of esteem the tradesmen of the district presented his little daughter, Miss Westbrook, with this magnificent toy. Wills and letters in the possession of its present owner, Mrs. Cyril Holland-Martin, show that it has passed through the hands of the female line of that family without interruption.

Mr. G. Bernard Hughes, chronicler of the history of the Westbrook Baby House,[1] gives the following detailed description:

"The Westbrook Baby House is an extremely handsome piece, and its design at once associates if with the chest-on-stand popular at the turn of the century. The house itself takes the place of the chest-of-drawers, and is mounted on a separate

[1] *Country Life,* October 19, 1951.

stand, 2 ft. $\frac{1}{2}$ in. high. Its six plinth-mounted legs consist of plain, tapering columns, heavily cupped and based, and topped by a deeply arched frieze of extremely solid construction, a style tending to lose favour from about 1710. The stand, like the house, is built from oak stained to a rich brown, brilliantly smooth with the patina of two-and-a-half centuries. Both are in their original condition, and no renovations have been needed.

"The baby house itself, measuring 3 ft. $7\frac{1}{2}$ ins. in width and 3 ft. 2 ins. to the ridge of the oak roof, represents a well-to-do home such as was being built in the main street of every town of the period. Its shallow roof is carved to simulate slates, and its handsome door—glazed, panelled and surrounded by pilasters and carved swan-neck pediment—is flanked by well-proportioned windows. The front is constructed with a central fixed panel containing a window and the front door. This opens into the hall.

"Apart from this central panel, the whole front of the house opens as two hinged doors containing the glazed windows of the four apartments, to which full access is thus obtained—dining-room and drawing-room to the right, kitchen and bedroom to the left.

"The handsome exterior is more than matched by all that is revealed when these doors are swung back. Here is a vivid study of the period that produced it, as most of the furniture, ornaments and even the tiny inhabitants originated at the same date. Here is walnut furniture in the style associated with fashionable living in Queen Anne's day—chairs, stools and tables with sturdy cabriole legs. The dining-room, uncarpeted in conformity with the fashion of the day, is furnished with table, stool, and three tall, splat-backed, deep-seated chairs. There is even a picture on the wall, framed in tortoiseshell, and a gilt-framed 'landscape' mirror above the fireplace, similar to that in the drawing-room above. Like in the drawing-room, the fireplace surround consists of hand-decorated cardboard squares in imitation of blue-painted Dutch tiles. The dining-room houses a miniature knife-box containing a complete set of cutlery with pistol-shaped handles of brass. This was probably introduced to the baby house later in the century.

"The drawing-room floor is covered with a hand-embroidered carpet: pile carpets were unfashionable during the Queen Anne and early Georgian periods. The chairs are tall, single chairs like those of the dining-room, but they have upholstered backs in rich brocades. Particularly notable is the circular card-table—an indispensable piece of furniture at that time—which folds across the the centre on concealed iron hinges. Appropriately the drawing-room houses an exceptionally interesting item and one which the original small owner would recognise as a miniature version of the kind of work she herself might be expected to produce. This is a cabinet japanned and decorated with carved ivory and containing some petit-point embroidery in silk, some of it unfinished. This cabinet, mounted on a cabriole-legged stand, is a rare example of such work in miniature. Suspended from the centre of the ceiling is another extremely rare toy, a six-candle chandelier of silver, with its branches curving from a polished reflecting-ball of solid silver.

"Adjoining this room is the bedroom, dominated by a ceiling-high tester bed, complete with draw curtains and quilted bed-cover. In the fashion of its period, every part of the bed is fabric-covered, and the pale blue damask silk conveys the correct impression of magnificence. Indicative of the care lavished on each detail in the furnishing of this house is the fact that the bed's rectangular framework is pierced for the cords that would be woven in and out to support the mattress. The floor is covered with a carpet worked in gros-point. The veneered chest-of-drawers is packed with dolls' clothing. The drawer knobs are of turned brass screwed into the wood. On top is a pincushion, its greatest measurement less than an inch. The chest-of-drawers, as was customary in Queen Anne's day, is accompanied by a wall mirror in an arch-topped gilt frame. To complete any small girl's delight, the room also includes a cradle. This is of wicker, then fashionable, and made extremely decorative by dainty needlework.

"In many ways the most fascinating room, now as throughout the life of the baby house, is the kitchen. The ceiling-high oak dresser and the spit rack on the fire are affixed to the walls, but a wonderful assortment of further equipment brings the room to life. The spit above the fireplace is thrust through a model goose. The fireplace opening contains a portable grate such as was then replacing the old fire-basket with dogs and creepers. There are copper pans hanging at the side of the dresser, hammered from the solid plate and tinned. On the table is a tiny marble mortar.

"The dolls and their clothing appear to be mainly contemporary with the baby house, except where the original wooden heads have required renewal. These figures in their rich and varied costumes, add greatly to the charm of their surroundings."

Until the reign of George III baby houses were exclusively the toys of a privileged class. From then onwards they were sold in the shops and their popularity grew. They took their place side by side with English-made grocers' shops and butchers' shops (108) which had a novel appeal for boys, whereas milliners' and dressmakers' counters were intended for girls (72). From the beginning of the twentieth century factory-made dolls' houses were turned out to meet the demand of the lower-income groups. Before the 1914 war, dolls' houses were sold in a range varying from the cheap wooden-box type (one and a half feet high) with cardboard furniture to the richly furnished mansion, complete with carpets and silverware.

These houses are microcosmic indications of the trends in domestic architecture, for they have moved from the Edwardian red-brick dwelling-house to the country cottage with roses round the door; from the suburban villa, with side garage and red-tiled roof, to the detached spacious home in its own grounds; from the functional apartment-block, with its streamlined and tubular furniture, to the maisonette.

A serious attempt to carry into the future the pattern of English life of 1920 was the famous dolls' house presented to H.M. Queen Mary[1] as a token of national goodwill in 1924. Widespread public interest was aroused by this wonderful model, scaled at one inch to the foot, to which the leading artisans and manufacturers contributed

[1] Designed by Sir Edwin Lutyens, O.M., 1869-1945.

85. Wax doll, unusually dressed as an old woman, *c.* 1800

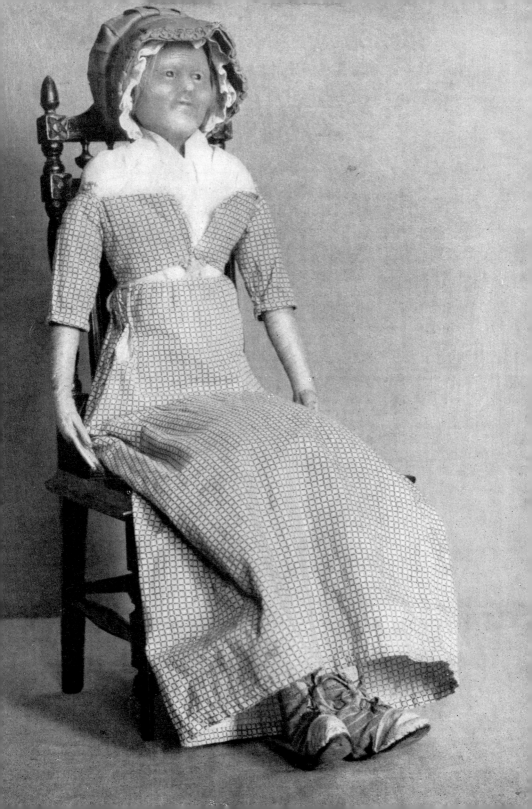

86. The Tate Baby House, 1760, at Bethnal Green Museum, London
87. Early Victorian dolls' villa — with metal balcony

samples of their products worked out to the finest detail. It was a challenge to British workmansip to maintain this perfect scale as uniform. Coats of paint had to be reduced to one-twelfth the normal thickness; pipes had to be reduced to a minimum to permit water to fow through them. Clocks were made to tick and chime; doors to lock; heating installation to give warm water; books, printed in minuscule type and bound beautifully in leather, could be read by aid of a magnifying glass. Queen Mary's Dolls' House, as it is generally known, has been described by connoisseurs as being "so perfect as to seem incredible."[1]

88. Playing with dolls. *From Gregor and Von Sydow's "Leishens Puppenstube,"* 1884

We have observed how the Germans, as in all their play-techniques disposed to be highly methodical, worked out an approach to doll-play as systematical as it was logical.

Distinct from the game of "Home," based on the different rooms in the model residence, they produced separate toy kitchens which

---

[1] *Dolls and Dolls' Houses* (Victoria and Albert Museum Booklet No. 16).

were accurate replicas of the well-equipped rooms in which the *Hausfrau* spent so much of her life. These were known as "Nuremberg Kitchens" and in the mid-nineteenth century were splendidly fitted with small stove, pots and pans hanging from appropriate hooks, jars and canisters, and cooking utensils of every type. They were made from copper or pewter, like the domestic articles, but some wooden crocks were also manufactured in the regions where wooden toys were the convention.

89. A wicker doll's perambulator, *c.* 1870. *From Gregor and Von Sydow's* *"Leishens Puppenstube,"* 1884

The toy kitchen became fashionable in France, where makers imitated the Nuremberg kitchens, surmounting them with a small signboard labelled *Cuisine.* The kitchen game came to England, and by the nineteenth century the tiny utensils were made mostly of tin. The usual pattern of doll-play was for the small child to act as cook or mother, seat the dolls around the table and serve meals in the way customary to the home. The meal-time conventions were dramatised, table manners and etiquette became the subject of conversation between child and toys, and in this way the Dolls' Tea Party, the Reception of Guests, became a natural function of the play-technique.

Concentration on baby-care and mothercraft led to the production of miniature vehicles in which small dolls were wheeled along the floor for their daily outing. The resemblance which these bassinets, baby-carriages, push-cars and cradles-on-wheels bear to the real ones is a remarkable example of the thoroughness with which the German artisans copied the originals (89). Those doll-carriages in the Bethnal Green Museum, made from straw, wood and metal, are meticulous copies of the real article and give fascinating accuracy in much detail. Their workmanship is equalled only by the bedroom furniture and washing sets produced at that same period (90).

By the year 1850, together with the Christmas Tree and the Easter Bunny, dolls' tea-sets and dinner-services from Germany were capturing the imagination of all good little girls everywhere. They were faithful replicas; they were inexpensive; and the pleasure to be derived from extending a collection, little by little, seemed boundless. Some sets were made of good porcelain—the majority of china-clay, either rough or glazed; these were augmented by miniature glassware pieces from Bohemia, and a passing vogue of ivory furniture which came from Chima, and later, from Japan. The Russian dolls' furniture in the main resembles the German prototypes, *i.e.* lathe-turned utensils of polished wood, showing the grain, and larger sets from softwood, gaily painted and varnished.

The illustrations of French and Italian dolls' houses show that similar trends were followed, but in the finer examples it is Renaissance designs that are, naturally, in evidence.

In England the owner of a baby house would sometimes spend long hours at home making miniature furnishings. A more common practice was to give orders for miniatures to the same craftsmen who specialised in the production of the full-sized article. Thus a cabinet-maker was commissioned to make furniture, a pewterer or copper-smith to make kitchen tankards and coppers, and a silversmith to make miniature objects in silver for the dining- or drawing-room.[1]

Mrs. Jackson has concluded that all the silver miniatures dating from the Restoration were intended to be toys.[2] A large number of silver miniatures now in English private collections, although reproducing a Queen Anne pattern, were made in Holland. Acrobats, silver coaches drawn by horses, soldiers, sedan-chairs and curiosities are exclusively Dutch in origin.

Research into the distinctions dividing English from Dutch silver toys, undertaken by Charles Oman, has established, among other facts, the interesting evidence that English silver toys were always utensils, never human or animal figures. In a comprehensive essay on this subject Mr. Oman has pointed out also that only a small propor-

[1] G. Bernard Hughes, *The Westbrook Baby House.*
[2] *Toys of Other Days.*

tion of the so-called toys were small enough to fit into any ordinary dolls' house. His thesis is that the objects were intended to be the particular possessions of larger dolls. "In the best furnished nurseries the dolls were endowed with at least some sort of plate used downstairs by the master and mistress of the house."[1] One of the tankards

90. Doll's bedroom furniture, *c.* 1870. *From Gregor and Von Sydow's "Leishens Puppenstube,"* 1884

(in the Victoria and Albert Collection) is engraved with a coat-of-arms, which, although it might not be approved by the College of Arms, "is convincing enough to satisfy a child unlearned in heraldic lore." He further comments that tankards have been found "rudely engraved with initials in the manner customary for a husband and wife," and ascribes these pathetic relics to forms of doll-play in which the wedding ceremony was seriously enacted.

It seems natural that silversmiths proud of their work would, from time to time, delight in making smaller editions of the tankards and salvers which they wrought for special clients. In London they vied with each other towards the end of the seventeenth century, and some of them struck their wares, usually several times, with an individual stamp. Oman comments that prior to 1697 it is impossible to find a clue to a silversmith's identity, as the records are missing from Goldsmiths' Hall, but after that date the task becomes less difficult.

The Victoria and Albert Collection is divided into two sections; silver toys of Dutch origin and silver toys of English make. Experts in silver plate will find a comparison of the two styles in-

[1] *Apollo Miscellany* 1950: p. 15, English Silver Toys.

91. Dolls' house accessories, ranging from items dated 1720 to those of 1880, from the Gordon Hand Collection

92. Dolls' house furniture of Japanese canework, c. 1900

93. English farm and farmhouse, *c.* 1912. (By courtesy of Mrs. Alison Uttley)

94. Dutch inlaid chest-of-drawers and taper sticks, *c.* 1750; cane chair, *c.* 1800
95. Part of the Joyce Holt Collection, Westmorland

structive and fascinating. A kettle and stand, made in Dublin about 1760, is four and a half inches high. A fire-grate complete with irons, bearing a London mark of 1740, stands two and three-quarter inches in height. It is of special interest to find that the cheap fireplace and fire-iron sets, made from lead or zinc alloy about 1910, were in fact good imitations of these superb designs.

Replicas of many household utensils now no longer used are included in this collection. Particular mention should be made of the miniature wine-taster (1660); the "molionet" and chocolate-pot (1720); the plate-rack of the same date; and the silver snuffers and pan, maker G.M. of London, 1684–1685.

Other than these, a variety of porringers, cutlery sets, candle-sticks, tankards, mugs, teapots, coffee-pots and sugar-bowls, each reflect in miniature those subtleties and points in design which connoisseurs of old silver regard as having historical significance.

The makers of some of the precious silver miniatures contained in the Westbrook Baby House previously mentioned are on record. The fireplace and creepers, tongs, shovel and poker are struck with the London hallmark for 1718, and the silversmith who made them is registered at Goldsmiths' Hall under the name of John Clifton.

It was he who, according to G. B. Hughes' account of the House, was also responsible for the pair of silver tazzas, the hand-raised saucepan and the Warwick cruet with its three casters and two bottles.

An uncommon article which John Clifton made is a silver foot-stove of a kind used in wealthy families, "to laye under their feet while they do write, or studie, in cold weather, or in their couches to keep their feete warm."

The Charles II type chairs, which were produced in extravagant numbers when silver was everywhere in use, bear the mark of one Mat Madden, registered in 1696. Other notable items in the Westbrook Baby House are a three-legged pot by Thomas Ewesday and a spice-dredger with a London date-letter for 1727.

Silver dishes have never been the toys of the middle-class child. In her dolls' house play she has derived as much pleasure and fulfilment from miniature versions made out of lead filigree or of stamped tin. An examination of the miscellany of dolls' crockery, ornaments and tableware assembled in the Bethnal Green Museum's showcases proves that all kinds of material have at different periods been acceptable. Oddments have survived from tea-sets of Stafford pottery originating in 1830; glossy vases and bowls made in cream-coloured

Irish beleek; sets of wood from Austria and the Black Forest; pressed-tin willow-patterns from Japan; English stoneware or glazed china with red roses on them; fragile blown-glassware of fine texture and delicate shape; coarse clay or enamelled tin; natural objects like acorn-cups, walnut-shells or carefully sewn hides. All these diminutive toys persuade us that if the family table is the centre-piece of civilised home life, this fact has a strong intuitive attraction for the female child. She has a natural feeling that the artistic completeness of her doll's complicated "life-pattern" cannot be realised without the accessories appropriate to eating, bathing, dressing and resting. Of all the rituals contributing to the extensive and universal repertoire of doll-dramas, the act of tasting bread and wine is (to judge from the urge that drives children to make cups and dishes from tinfoil or cardboard) possibly the most deeply rooted manifestation in the spontaneous acts of self-expression through play.

As the focus in our society switches over from ordered family life, with its routines, its sense of security and the importance laid on each family occupying a house to itself, to more erratic patterns of community living, we find that the demand for dolls' houses and their small accessories recedes. This surely is a sign of the times. It is, on the other hand, encouraging to note from sales statistics that even if there has been a drop in the demand for toy houses, the salesgraph for children's babies maintains a steady level, if not a rising curve. It may be conjectured that as the housing of the population returns to normal, there will accordingly be a return to toys which are designed to emulate normal domestic life in its basic and richest aspects.

VI

WAR-PLAY AND TOY SOLDIERS

GAMES of combat have not changed greatly during the history of mankind. A study of traditional games shows us that the strategy and organisation of battle have been preserved in children's play long after the weapons and techniques themselves have become obsolete. War games are closely allied to pursuit games, since the former are merely a variation of the animal hunt of which the latter are a dramatic enactment.[1]

When the bow and arrow ceased to have any military value, it was taken over entirely as a child's toy, and it is in the toyshop today (apart from the precincts of archery clubs) that one finds small replicas of that one-time formidable weapon. The expression of the herd-instinct among boys of a certain age invariably takes the form of war games. These have been fought in turn with wooden sword and paper peaked-cap; with busby and popgun; with spiked helmet and rifle; and, as weapons and ideas become more mechanised, with imitations of everything in the armoury of modern warfare.

In recent times war games and soldier-play have been criticised by educationalists as fostering a militaristic spirit, but psychologists, and those who have done special research into this question, have concluded that the inculcation of militarism is largely a matter of home environment and not a direct result of such game-patterns.

Contemporary engravings confirm that boys and girls together freely played at soldiers since the Napoleonic wars. Before then the sport was probably confined to boys, and was, in the main, an outdoor one. It was introduced to England by the Normans, who laid much stress upon war like pastimes. The mounted knight was a game-concept widely followed in fifteenth and sixteenth century England. Children played pick-a-back in a way directly modelled on the jousts and tournaments. The tourney, which was the popular adult pastime, was naturally imitated by children in Norman castles, and they were encouraged to excel in the saddle and with the lance. It is probable that at this period the hobby-horse became widespread as a toy. Gröber has cited the instance of the young King Louis II of Hungary

---

[1] *Children's Games*, pp. 16-20.

ordering an armourer to make two knights in tourney-array on wooden horses, showing that "the Emperor must have taken great pleasure in the game" when he was a child.[1] Some of these models were set up on low platforms, with a child at either end manoeuvring them, by strings or through leverage, while the spectators gathered round— the true Anglo-Norman origin of our table game involving contest.

Apart, therefore, from action games in which children in the roles of warriors actually play at war, the war-toy really began with such contrivances for perpetuating the codes of chivalry.

Contemporaneously in the courts of Europe, most of the man-on-horseback toys were of metal. Some were pull-toys, bronze knights drawn along on solid metal wheels. The majority were exquisite figures copied from the élite regiments of the various kingdoms, the work of silversmiths who executed these for the pleasure of small princes at a royal command. Silver, and sometimes gold, were the metals used, but there are instances of early examples in German museums made from lead.

Precious metals remained the prerogative of these noble sponsors until, towards the middle of the eighteenth century, Frederick the Great had set all Europe thinking about armies, and a Nuremberg tin-founder and pewterer named Andreas Hilpert began to turn out hand-made cavalrymen for general purchase. These were masterpieces of craftsmanship and each of the early pieces bore his initials. From then onwards the tin soldier and the lead soldier took their place among the other popular toys, and in many ways their histories are parallel.[2]

In the interval the wooden soldiers reigned supreme as the poorer child's "mercenaries." It began in the Thuringian forest-belts, the centre of the Continental wooden-toy industry. They were much bigger than the metal types, and in simplicity of design combined a primitive quality with a peasant feeling for the subject that was far from atavistic. These soldiers towards the middle of the nineteenth century enjoyed a great vogue in England, and are of the type illustrated by Gordon Craig and humorously called *Biffins*.[3] They are completely obsolete today, except for some imports from Denmark and Sweden which are larger, more self-conscious stylisations of the old peasant productions.

[1] Karl Gröber, *Children's Toys of Bygone Days*, p. 13.
[2] Theodor Hampe, *Der Zinnsoldat*, Berlin 1924.
[3] *Book of Penny Toys*.

Wooden soldiers were made during the long winters when the villages were snow-bound, and the villagers tried to make up for their loss of income by making wooden kitchen articles and toys. The latter included trees, houses, mills and steepled churches. They were all made of pinewood, sawn off and turned. The work of a knife could be seen only on the trees, which were made by chipping off thin layers of wood from the turned trunk. No other carving was done. The detail was painted in and afterwards brightly varnished. The English Redcoat was turned out complete with his black bearskin head-dress. Six soldiers were packed into a smooth, fragile box of matchwood, which sold for about two shillings. They were also brought to the markets of Vienna in the springtime, where the Slovak peasants spread them on their cloth bags and sold them to passers-by.

96. A landing-party of British sailors, with a breech-loading field-gun, *c.* 1890

A few toymakers concentrated on an output of larger and more realistic specimens made from plaster. Their breakable character made them unsuitable for floor-games, but some splendidly moulded examples have survived wear and tear. One is of French manufacture, and is a reproduction of a cavalry officer mounted on a charger in full gallop. His head rotates within a socket.

If the doll is the universal plaything for a girl, so is the toy soldier the natural toy for boys. Gröber has described the tin soldier as "a new thing which in a very short time was to conquer the world."

The first tin soldiers were called "lead." They were cast in soapstone and cut by artists from their own drawings. One German manufacturer specialised in casting a flat-tin variety, and these are still on the market, having persisted and maintained their popularity abroad as a cheaper line throughout several major wars and political upheavals. The German soldiers were mainly of solid metal. Hollow soldiers were an English invention. The innovation, which had the double advantage of lightness and portability, radically altered the manufacturing process, and soon German factories had turned completely from making solids, to the hollow type.

English children began playing with English-made soldiers about

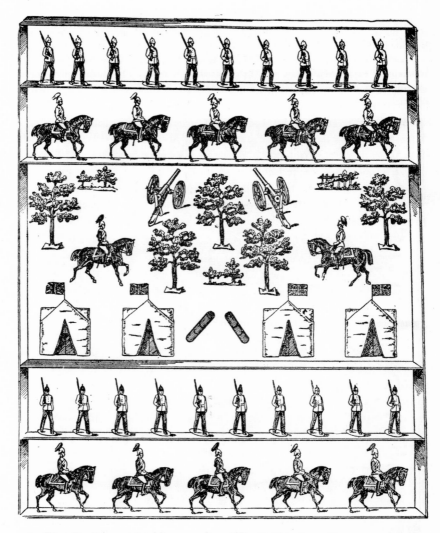

97. First English metal soldiers, *c.* 1890: "The British Army Encampment Set"

1868, the year when a toy-maker named Britain began to mould them and market them against German monopoly. The extent to which they have influenced the play-hours of British boys is vividly gathered from a descriptive memoir written by C. W. Beaumont.

"Of all the various kinds of presents that I received during the birthdays and Christmasses of my childhood I can recall none that afforded me greater delight than a box of toy soldiers, especially those of Britain's make. There was a definite thrill about the shiny red cardboard box in which they came, and another was provided when, the lid having been removed, one saw rows of soldiers fastened with a thread to a strip of cardboard to protect them from harm. There was yet another moment of excitement when, the threads having been cut, the soldiers were lifted out and set up one by one. How fresh and smart they looked in their shining uniforms of bright new paint."[1]

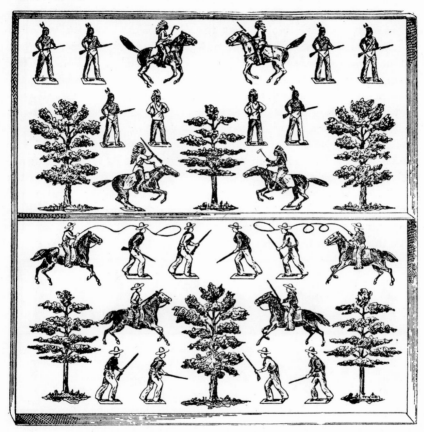

98. A set of cowboys and Indians, *c.* 1890

In the initial days of industrial struggle between the English firm and its German rivals, all was fair in trade- and toy-war. There was no protection against piracy, and the growing demand for the English series and styles led to imitation by Germany and Japan, which was the surest form of flattery, albeit menacing.

Early catalogues found among the records at Messrs. Britain's

[1] C. W. Beaumont, *Flashback, Stories of My Youth*, p. 101.

premises in Hornsey (once a dwelling-house but now one of a group of world-famous toy-soldier factories) confirms that the ranges of this toy have not altered substantially in half a century, when compared with other metal toys. The illustrated old price-lists give evidence that the Life Guards and Seaforth Highlanders remain as they were when first designed; that the Royal Marines and Dublin Fusiliers retain their pristine glory; that the Wild West cowboys, whether mounted or on foot, still are the most colourful imaginable (98, 99).

One group of soldiers, compiled as a tableau set, is entitled The Changing of the Guard. The box consists of the bandsmen, the colours, the Old Guard marching along and the New Guard presenting arms—eighty-three pieces in all. The majority of the Britain designs date from between 1910 and 1925, but this particular box was the maker's response to the coronation ceremony of 1937. The model was first produced in 1936 for the coronation of King Edward VIII, with a model of the King seated in the coach; but, upon the abdication, a new model of King George VI and his queen had quickly to be made. This was put in all further coaches. In addition they were sent out to all children who had already received coaches with the King alone inside.

99. A set of mounted cowboys, *c.* 1890

H. G. Wells, whose book *Little Wars* was inspired by soldier-play, believed that it is possible to play the great game of the world much as it is played over the territory of nations with death-dealing weapons and real men. On the floor of his room he would arrange scale-model countrysides with the aid of branches, cardboard bridges, chalked-out streams, rocks, and cardboard houses, forts, barracks. Before a battle began, his system provided that the general in each opposing army might dispose his forces without the enemy being aware of that disposirion. Thus a curtain was drawn between the two "warring" generals at the outset of each game.[1]

During the last two hundred years there has been a steady growth in the hobby of collecting miniature figures, of which the functional

[1] H. G. Wells, *Floor Games*, The Toys to Have, p. 3.

100. Pedal-propelled horse-on-wheels, real hide, from the French imperial nursery

origin once was exclusively that of a toy. The Czar Peter III of Russia was an enthusiastic collector. Other imperial monarchs who pursued this interest were Louis XII and Louis XIV; the last of the Russian Czars, who was supplied with ornate miniatures of his various Regiments of Guards; the ex-Emperor of Germany.

The Medici of Florence were among the Renaissance clients who ordered a series of contemporary figures from Nuremberg makers.

The number of collectors, as Otto Gottstein points out, has increased greatly during the past forty years.

"Societies, comprising many thousand of members, have been founded on the Continent, in England and in the United States. The exchange of figures has led to a demand for special types not so easily obtained, and thus a smaller circle of enthusiasts has been formed who have had their designs manufactured privately."

This exclusivity removes metal soldiers far from the sphere of toys and elevates them to the status of rare collectors' pieces, since all new models, before they are engraved and cast in the moulds, will have entailed the combined research of experienced artists, historians, modellers and engravers. The result of such collaboration is a species of metal figure similar in size and appearance to the older toy-soldier prototype, but comparable with the finest miniatures of medieval times, and, as might be expected, of ever-increasing monetary value.

The soldiers with which the author of *The New Machiavelli* and *The Outline of History* amused himself were simple tin soldiers. The floor needed for soldier-play must be "covered with linoleum or cork carpet, so that toy soldiers will stand up upon it, and of a colour and surface that will take and show chalk-marks."

Later on in this unusual treatise, when he has become quite absorbed and carried away by his zest for his subject, Wells goes on to digress for a moment on his favourite topic:

"Let me now say a little about toy soldiers and the world to which they belong. They used to be flat, small creatures in my own boyhood, in comparison with the magnificent beings one can buy today. There has been an enormous improvement in our national physique in this respect. Now they stand nearly two inches high and look you broadly in the face, and they have the movable arms and alert intelligence of scientifically exercised men. You get five of them mounted or nine afoot in a box for tenpence-halfpenny. We like those of British manufacture best; other makes are of incompatible sizes. We have a rule that saves much trouble. All red coats belong to F. R. W. and all coloured coats to G. P. W.... Also we have sailors; but, since there are no red-coated sailors, blue counts as red."[2]

[1] Prince John of Löwenstein, *Proclaim Freedom*, 1952.
[2] H. G. Wells, *Floor Games*, p. 15.

01. Noah's Ark and animals of painted wood, French or Italian, *c.* 1850

102. A set of Boy Scouts containing figures with movable arms, a tree, a gate and hurdles. The Boys can climb into eight different positions in the tree, swing on the gate, mount the hurdles and assume many other positions that the ingenuity of the possessor may suggest. (From a catalogue, *c.* 1910)

The remarkable philosopher who systematised soldier-play in such a charming way then comments upon the other similar toys which are played with alongside the marching men, such as Beefeaters, Red Indians and Zulus, "for whom there are special rules." He does not omit to mention the metal dogs, cats, lions, tigers, horses, camels, cattle and elephants of a corresponding size, which add to the possibilities for imaginative play.

The latter, manufactured in lead after soldiers had established themselves in the nursery, are really metal afterthoughts, in the shape of farmyard and jungle sets, on the traditional Noah's Ark toy (which was always made of wood, not metal), together with the pairs of animals that go with it. Noah's Ark, with its folding-back roof and brightly painted animals, follows the same design in most European countries. Of German origin, it is believed to have been a speciality of the Oberammergau peasants, and indeed, with its Biblical associations, this it the sort of folk-toy that might be expected to have evolved in such an atmosphere. It had a sabbatical function in nineteenth-century England, where children had "Sunday dolls," and were allowed to play with the Ark, and to place the animals around the floor in a special "Sunday game" (101). Dickens, incidentally, has written that some of these Noah's Arks presented to "birds and beasts an uncommonly tight fit. I assure you they would be crammed in anyhow at the roof, and rattled into the smallest compact."

In some countries, rubber is now cast into toy soldiers; while plastic materials have immense possibilities, both for colour and accuracy in shape. Paper and cardboard also had their heyday, when lithography was applied to toy manufacture. Soldiers prepared from sugar-candy and jelly, like the Easter egg, are an extension of the toy into gastronomic fields, whereas the phenomenon of the chocolate soldier is something that compares with the also-disappearing bullseye, candy-sugar and butterscotch confections which were in such demand between the wars.

The modern equivalent of lead, which is a variety of zinc composition, still heads the list as the most acceptable material. It is from this that the adult collector's model soldiers are also made.

All foregoing three quotations by English writers refer to the kind of soldier at which the healthy lad roars "Bang! Bang!" as, with his cane or cannon-ball, he lays devastation and carnage among his diminutive legions. Very different is the attitude of adult collectors to that of the enthusiast of pediarchic play. The latter is content to call his soldiers "toys"; the former insists that they are "models." Just as the layman, in his innocence and ignorance, frequently confuses toy sailing-boats with scale-model watercraft, so does he allow himself to be confounded by the similarity in appearance between toy soldiers and their patrician superiors, which are essentially collectors' pieces. Enlightenment on major points, as on the more subtle distinctions, may be sought through the Model Soldier Clubs which exist in all countries where this form of collecting has become an educative and eclectic hobby.

Possessor of a magnificent collection is the Secretary of the British Model Soldier Society, Mr. A. G. Clayton. He has explained that there is a dearth of reference books on this subject, but that through the publication of the Society's magazine and sporadic essays in various organs, the basis for a history of the hobby is being laid. Women and juniors are also on the membership roll of the Model Soldier Society, which comprises rich and poor, artisans and retired people, clergymen and industrialists—all sharing a common passion for this interest which demonstrates how a trend in play while young may, in later years, grow into a form of play of a much higher intellectual order.

The British Society has on its books such outstanding collections as that owned by Mr. P. D. Connett, who specialises in ancient soldiery, his historical range dating from 3000 B.C. to the armies of Trajan Rome. Another world-famous collection is that assembled over many years by the late Mr. Otto Gottstein of London. He collected the "continental flat" type, on which he was the leading world authority. This collector was responsible for the military tableaux at the Royal United Services Institute Museum, located in the Banqueting Hall, in Whitehall—superb dioramas which have attracted visitors from all over the world, including military experts who were trained in the use of models for positional manoeuvres, while studying at Staff Colleges and Military Academies.

A particularly fine set of models was made specially for a window display by one of the oldest English firms carrying on this rare and picturesque trade. The establishment, just off London's Cambridge Circus, was that of Messrs. Henry Potter, makers for a considerable period of military musical instruments at this address. The production of bandsmen's drums and brass instruments of all kinds is a highly skilled craft, one which is becoming increasingly

103. Solid lead soldier, *cuirassier*, height 17 cms., in the Musée de l'Armée, Pari

uncommon, as mechanised warfare is dispensing with the customary pageantry and colour of the infantry bands. The display showed a set of Grenadier Bandsmen, in marching formation, arranged on a wooden stand. The period is 1790, and the models here displayed, amid the trappings, regimental insignia and varnished drums, were copied from a rare print depicting the original soldiers which hangs inside this shop where so much of the romance of soldiering is concentrated.

Since the invention of the tank for battle there has been a tendency to replace toy soldiers with scale models of the apparatus actually used in present-day warfare, which brings the design of toys directly into line with the design of real weapons. By this means the process whereby military toys were always slightly in arrears of martial innovations has been brought to an end, and children now play with the last word in destructive equipment. Accordingly, the massing of armies of toy soldiers has been superseded by armoured divisions.

The ambulance and stretcher-bearer, which were a mark of the 1914-1918 lead-soldiers war-set, have now been outsted by armoured cars, anti-aircraft batteries, motor-cycle units and parachute-troops dropped by aircraft. By pressing buttons and switches the small boy of today can galvanise his wheeled and motorised forces into action. It is matter for speculation whether he derives as positive a stimulus as that which H. G. Wells promised in his concluding sentences of *Floor Games*, when he summed up his purpose in advocating informal and improvised combat:

"This time I set out merely to tell of the ordinary joys of playing with the floor, and to gird improvingly and usefully at toy-makers. So much, I think, I have done. If one parent or one uncle buys the wiselier for me, I shall not altogether have lived in vain."

04. Lead soldiers, 29 cms. high, played with by imperial princes of France, Château de Compiègne Collection

VII

"BAA LAMBS TO SELL"

"THE shopkeeper, seeing in me a likely convert and potential customer, assumed the most winning tones and explained to me how the scenes were cut out and mounted on cardboard, the manner in which the figures were cut out, fixed on tin stands, and pushed on, or drawn off, the stage by means of a long wire. Warming to the subject he imparted to me the secret of simulating lightning by blowing lycopodium through a candle flame, the tremendous possibilities in the skilful use of coloured fires, which revelations roused my covetousness to such a point that I would willingly have parted with the clothes I wore in order to be the master of such joys. Perhaps, one day, there will be a new version of *Dr. Faustus* in which Mephistopheles, disguised as the proprietor of a toy-shop, succeeds in gaining the former's soul in exchange for a model theatre complete, of course, with all accessories."[1]

It is difficult to determine just where to trace the borderline between toys proper and that whole paraphernalia of a schoolboy's life contained within the trade description "Jokes, Tricks, Novelties and Puzzles." At such a point there arise problems more vexing than anything Euclid tried to solve: then must all-important decisions be taken as to whether a postal order should be invested in number 2383 of the catalogue; or allocated to a booklet entitled *Fifty Amusing Toys and How to Make Them*; or, yet, on such irresistible items temptingly sketched to answer the descriptions of rubber peanuts, musical fish, barking dog, dancing devil, snake-in-the-egg or Japanese flowers.

Occasionally, the latest gadget will be announced with a name that spellbinds the youthful investor whose pocket-money by now has only one purpose—a novelty, say, like the nervo-graph?

When, during my own schooldays, we used to meet at the Bourse of Gadgetry, we had clearly cut ideas. "Ellisden's for Novelties — Davenport's for Magic" was our formula.

It was in August 1898 that Lewis Davenport opened a small shop in the Mile End Road, opposite the People's Palace. This he devoted to Magic. It was not long before young Lewis sold his magic in the shop by day and performed his magic in the place of entertainment across the way by night. Only the initiated today know about, and call at, the shop in Great Russell Street, with its legacy of Fifty Years in Magic, where the Davenport family carries on its unique

[1] C. W. Beaumont, *Flashback, Stories of My Youth.*

and wonderful business. Mr. Gilly Davenport is perhaps the only man in England who is entitled to describe himself professionally as a "joke manufacturer."

From this research laboratory, where are analysed ingredients of the sense of the comic, one is told that according to Mr. Davenport's experience the nation least blessed with a sense of humour are the Germans. "Anything except a false nose is beyond them." Indians, by contrast, prefer a puzzle, anything solemn and intricate; the French, it was observed, favour joke-toys bordering on the impolite.

Not many boys who receive through the post such wicked engines as the "spilt ink" bottle with a "celluloid blot," exploding cigarette, or infuriating devices called rubber "plate-lifters," discover until much later in life shelves packed with mystery and magic, shrouded in shadows in this temple of the prank.

What the Big Top is to the circus votary, or the taxidermist's window to the young naturalist, or magic casements to the poet Keats, so is the toyshop to the average child. One often feels that the town-bred boy and girl of today, whose almanac is illuminated by one carnival-day, the annual visit to the modern emporium with its fabulous displays at Christmas-time, never reach the hidden world behind glass panes which is presented continually to those who live in the smaller towns and villages. The village toyshop, hallowed and time-honoured, and kept by a personage as omnipotent as he or she is familiar, is the natural Mecca of all those who press noses against a window-pane.

It is a characteristic phenomenon of our society that the old-time toyshop is passing away, with its shelves and counters overladen with all sorts of traditional things. Since 1939 fewer stores are devoted entirely to the sale of toys and nothing else; and the tendency is for toys to become "a department" in a great store or share room-space with such companions as hardware, tobacco or stationery. Still, in the imaginations of those who knew the romance of older days live for ever the *boutiques fantasques* of yesteryear.

In medieval times, pedlars hawked home-made toys through England's fairs and market-places. Many large towns, until the last war, had their allotted places where toys could be bought from street-traders. The very term "cheapjack" derives from hawkers who sold their wares in this way, and some Londoners will retain memories of them taking up their pitches in lines, at such recognised marts as the pavement near Messrs. Gamages, at Holborn Circus, or at the North Gate entrance to Regent's Park, on Sundays. Their colourful trade still survives today on the street-barrows, or with the balloon man. One remembers, not so very long ago, the rag-bone-and-bottle men who offered paper windmills and balloons as barter for stone jam-jars, the quality of their wares being scaled to the size and value of the jam-pot tendered.

Many Londoners recall women pedlars who sold woolly lambs on a tray, and whose ancient street-cry was a familiar slogan:

> "Baa-lambs to sell, baa-lambs to sell
> I've got white pretty baa-lambs to sell."

The words found under the engraving by Tempest of an English toy-pedlar, *c.* 1692, run:

> *"Troops every one*
> *Chevaux pour les enfants,"*

the toy horses portrayed here being no longer made.

An illustration of boys demonstrating dancing dolls is perhaps more intriguing. It tells the story of Italian lads who came to London from Sicily and, by their effrontery, annoyed the Cockneys, who put them in their place by soundly thrashing them.

The toy-booth was a feature of the seventeenth and eighteenth centuries, and in the old bill depicting a Frost Fair on the River Thames in the winter of 1715-1716 is seen one of the gaily tented counters devoted to the sale of toys.

Few modern artists have caught the spirit of the old-fashioned toy-shop so fully as Wyndham Payne, who illustrated C. W. Beaumont's toy stories, *The Wonderful Journey* and the *Strange Adventures of a Toy Soldier*.

Toyshops which exercised a lasting influence upon children destined to achieve greatness in the history of Britain were those that concentrated on the Juvenile Drama. This form of play was pursued as a mimetic activity through toys patterned on the rococo style and structure of the Regency theatres.

Toy Theatres, as they were called, have enriched the boyhood of writers as different in outlook as Charles Dickens, G. K. Chesterton and Sir Winston Churchill. Working with these miniatures seems to have had a spell-binding appeal, and visits to the shops that sold them were regarded as pilgrimages, kindling the imagination. No subtler testimony in literature to such experiences exists than in

Robert Louis Stevenson's essay which he, an enthusiast for the hobby, published in *The Magazine of Art of 1884*.

"There stands, I fancy to this day (but now how fallen!) a certain stationer's shop at a corner of the wide thoroughfare that joins the city of my childhood with the sea. When, upon any Saturday we made a party to behold the ships, we passed that corner; and since in those days I loved a ship as a man loves Burgundy or daybreak, this of itself has been enough to hallow it. But there was more than that. In the Leith Walk window, all the year round, there stood displayed a theatre in working order, with a forest 'set', a 'combat' and a few 'robbers carousing' in the slides; and below and about, dearer tenfold to me! the plays themselves, those budgets of romance, lay tumbled one upon another. Long and often have I lingered there with empty pockets ... it was a giddy joy. That shop, which was dark and smelt of Bibles, was a loadstone rock for all that bore the name of boy."[1]

In its earliest form the Toy Theatre evolved from the Peepshow— a kind of mobile cabinet popular during the seventeenth century in France and Italy, and carried by "the peepshow men." By the mid-eighteenth century these travelling showmen had become a recognised attraction at English fairs and festivals. Then there arose the juvenile slogan which was to persist for a century afterwards—"A penny for the peepshow." Sometimes the entertainment offered was accompanied by music on the hurdy-gurdy or the concertina.

A book published in 1785 contains the following verse describing a picture of a show in progress:

"This box does pleasant sight enclose
And landscape and perspective shows
Of every varied sort.
A penny is the price I ask
For execution of my task
And I get a penny for't."

Toy theatres reached their zenith of popularity about 1840. For half a century after that date they were sold in certain old-fashioned shops. By the 'eighties they were beginning to lose their appeal for children, although up to the 1890's there were still a very few—one, notably, at Margate—which catered for the juvenile market.

Two of the most famous London shops were in Hoxton, an area described by A. E. Wilson,[2] the authoritative historian of toy theatres, as "a dingy hinterland of North London, with its roaring traffic,

---

[1] *A Penny Plain and Twopence Coloured*, illustrated by Victorian woodcuts; Introduction by Barry Duncan (Thule Press, 1948).
[2] A. E. Wilson, *Penny Plain, Twopence Coloured* (Harrap, 1932).

POT
NEW IMPROV

London, Published by B Po

To be used Flat or Built

105. Regency stage front from a

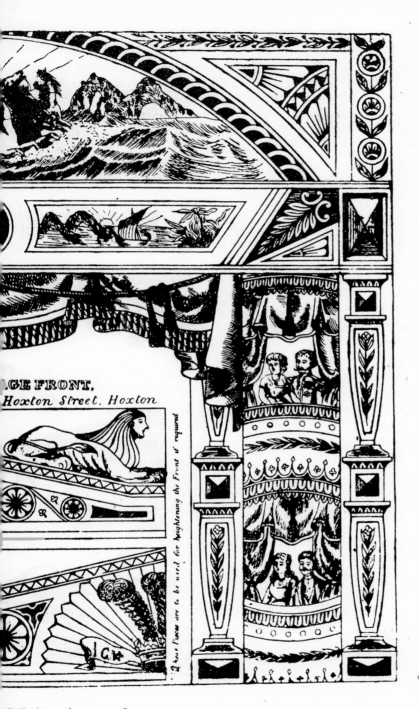

GE FRONT.

Hoxton Street. Hoxton

These Pieces are to be used for heightening the Front if required

Pollock toy theatre, *c.* 1870

shabby warehouses and narrow, murky, forbidding side-streets."
Yet for all its dreariness, the district attracted like a Mecca "in which
the two shops engaged in friendly rivalry, presided over by the arch-
priests—Webb and Pollock . . ."

Webb's shop was at 49 Old Street, St. Luke's. Benjamin Pollock
plied his trade at 73 Hoxton Street, known as "the Old Curiosity Shop
of the Juvenile Drama," until a flying-bomb destroyed the site during
the last war. These two men were living links with an unbroken
tradition of toy-theatre firms, dealers and engravers who bore the
names of Hodgson, Jameson and West (109), and the more famous
name of Skelt, for whose exotic style of design R. L. S. coined his
playful term of *skeltery*.

At these shops the sets were sold in the form of sheets to be painted,
cut out, pasted and, with the aid of a boy's time-honoured paraphernalia, transformed from a state of prefabricated flatness into
the three-dimensional marvel of a tiny playhouse (105, 106). The operation provided lessons in handicraft, theatricals, elocution, engineering
and aesthetics in a combination which few twentieth-century toys can
emulate. The sheets, outlined in black on white, were sold for one
penny; and for twice that sum, hand-coloured, transfigured won-
drously with crimson lake, Prussian blue and Tyrian purple. In that
choice between two qualities originates the catchphrase, now a current
idiom in our speech, of "penny plain, twopence coloured."

Webb and Pollock productions now exist in private collections and
are much sought after. The most extensive and impressive range of
toy-theatre prints, published between 1811 and 1850, were assembled
by a London lawyer, Mr. Ralph Thomas, who based his fastidious
collecting on a priceless nucleus originally held by a Mr. Frederick
Hodgetts. Both lots, comprising five large albums, were presented to
the British Museum and may there be viewed at the Prints and
Drawing Department.

When set up for a show the toy theatre was a thing of true colour
and romance (107).

"Its boxes were filled with guests, its orchestra posed for action. When all was
apparently in readiness behind the scenes, the candle footlights were lighted and the
curtain rolled up to reveal the characters standing woodenly in various positions
about the stage, and three or four times as large as the pictured audience. Then the
drama began, with the young stage manager reading the parts. Characters in their
tin slides would be moved across the stage and exit into the wings. The drama pro-
ceeded with many hitches such as failure of characters to appear when their turns
were spoken or wrong characters leaving the stage. Sometimes the entire structure

collapsed through the undue exertion of the stage hands. All this time the candle footlights would be requiring constant attention and giving off foul odours and soot. . . ."[1]

In the view of Mr. Wilson, with whom to discuss these rites is like learning about vintages from a wine-taster, all the pleasure lay in the preparation. The preliminary delights sprang from going to select, and then paying for, the prints; from colouring them to one's liking; from planning the effects—grains of Epsom salts sprinkled on cotton-wool for the snow scenes, special powders for the explosions, clattering tin trays for storms—all the manoeuvrings that boys enjoy with glue and paste-pot, with wood and brushes, with the dreadfully smelly oil which fed the wick. R. L. S. speaks of "the boy doating on these bundles of delight," and of "the physical pleasure in the sight and touch of them which he would jealously prolong."

In a memoir of Charles Dickens by his son we are given a glimpse of the novelist's love of the society of children, through an account of his share, with his friend Clarkson Stanfield, the Royal Academician, in the making of a toy theatre and the production of an original piece at his home in Devonshire Terrace:

"This I remember was a spectacle called *The Elephant of Siam* and its production on a proper scale of splendour necessitated the designing and painting of several new scenes which resulted in such a competition between my father and Stanfield that you would have thought their very existences depended on the mounting of the same elephant. And even after Stanfield had had enough of it, my father was still hard at work and pegged away at the landscapes and architecture of Siam with an amount of energy which in any other man would have been extraordinary, but which I soon learned to look upon as quite natural in him. This particular form of dramatic fever wore itself out after the piece was produced, I remember, and the theatre— much to my delight, for I had hitherto had but little to do with it, found its way to the nursery, where in process of time a too realistic performance of *The Miller and His Men*, comprising an injudicious expenditure of gunpowder and red-fire, brought about the catastrophe which finishes the career of most theatres and very nearly set fire to the house as well. . . ."[2]

It is remarkable that *The Miller and His Men*, most universal in its appeal, should have been the tragedy through the enactment of which so many cherished toys literally went up in smoke. It was ever so. For a later generation the story is repeated in the reminiscences of C. B. Cochran, who confesses how it was that same drama which nipped his ardour when he was a boy of nine:

[1] Freeman, *Cavalcade of Toys*, Toy Theatres, pp. 299-309.
[2] *Daily News*, May 15, 1895.

". . . In working up to the climax, with revolving windmill, red-fire and so on, I felt the lack of four or more hands. Pushing on a character in a tin slide, lighting the red-fire, manipulating a trap and working the wheel, while at the same time speaking the lines of the characters, made me lose my presence of mind. . . . The character in the tin slide caught fire; the flames spread to the wings; I burnt my hand, and then the great conflagration! My theatre was reduced to ashes. . . ."[1]

Contending that conflagration was the usual fate of the toy dramas long before the play ended, A. E. Wilson explained to me that he was challenged by another enthusiast, Mr. D. L. Murray (a former editor of *The Times Literary Supplement* and himself owner of toy-theatre and toy-soldier collections). It was thus that an invitation was extended to the "Gibbon of Juvenile Drama" to visit his challenger's home in Lewes, there to witness a performance in which the final curtain would be reached without mishap. The author was entranced by a show in which the lines were spoken by professional actors, the incidental music provided by a gramophone, and stage lighting and management carried out by a competent team of experts. A memorable entertainment indeed, but as the guest remarked, far removed from the potentialities of a schoolboy manager of the 'nineties who worked single-handed or with only a friend's help!

Few students of toy-theatre history have succeeded in recapturing the atmosphere and oddity of those dealers' shops as well as D. L. Murray, who must be unique in having laid the first episodes of a novel in such a shop situated in Greensleeves Row, Clerkenwell. It seems certain that the eccentric Mr. O. Fawkes, a thinly disguised fictional personage, must have been known to many in the flesh:

" . . Mark then beheld a glimmer of small leaded panes, behind which gesticulating figures in tinsel and forests and palaces of an incredibly gay colouring, shone with a magical brilliance, a half-circle of ragged children hopping defiantly on the paving stones; and on the flight of three steps that led up to the glass door of the shop, a little old man with hair falling on his shoulders and an apron tied askew round his waist.

—Go away, he roared, the shop's closed.
—Ve vants our play fust.
—What play?
—*Sixteen-stringed Jack*, I tell yer!
—You can't have that one. It's out of print.
—Yer lie. It's in the winder there.
—I never take goods out of the window. . . ."[2]

Pennies invested in toy theatres were money well spent if we

[1] Preface to A. E. Wilson's *Penny Plain, Twopence Coloured* (Harrap, 1932).
[2] *Trumpeter, Sound!* p. 33 (Hodder and Stoughton, 1933).

reckon the number of children whose artistic education began in that way. "I must have spent a fortune on my hobby," declares C. B. Cochran," . . . in the 'eighties all my pocket-money went on sets of plays, my parents being generous because it kept me out of mischief." His keen interest in theatre was later shared, as he grew older,

106. Toy theatre cut-out sheet, *c.* 1840

with Aubrey Beardsley, the illustrator. Another outstanding artist and master of the poetic drama, Sacheverell Sitwell, has lamented with eloquent nostalgia the romantic era of the Harlequinade:

" . . I held some picture of that sort, always unsatisfied, at the back of my mind, until long after I had ceased to be a child. In fact, the vision was fulfilled only some ten years later when a chance remark led me to visit Mr. Pollock's shop in Hoxton. There, for the first time, one sees the romantic theatre in miniature form. . . . In a way it must have been a golden age of scene-painting. Timur the Tartar, one of the plays still sold, might well be Tamerlaine the Great. Yet its author was not Marlowe but 'Monk' Lewis. Alas! how many children have never heard of Hoxton and its juvenile drama. . . ."[1]

[1] Preface to *Flashback* (C. W. Beaumont).

It is entrancing to recall that along those same pavements, at one time or another, walked Gordon Craig, Lupino Lane, Sir Ralph Richardson; stars of the cinema, like Chaplin and Gladys Cooper; the impresario Diaghileff—all drawn mysteriously by the cardboard fancies first conceived as playthings for the young. The entire human stories of Pollock and West, those two specialists who were more than tradesmen ("consultants" would better describe their métier), are told with sympathy and feeling by A. E. Wilson in his canon reference of the subject of toy theatres. The author knew both these personages well, and being privileged to listen to him recall in anecdotes their attitudes to their calling makes one aware of an enchantment once veiled in darkest Hoxton that will be nevermore experienced. The prophetic import of his words, "when they are gone there will be nobody to carry on this ancient business. The famous firm of Reddington & Pollock will then be a legend," now rings like an epitaph. New conventions supplanted the Regency stage of which the toys were but replicas, for, when the adult drama took a different direction, the thing imitated in play became something else. They have died a natural death and are now merely museum pieces or the objects of collectors' quests.

As a plaything, the toy theatre survives in such cardboard cut-out games as the Punch and Judy set, which also retains the paper-covered booklet with the words, directions and dialogue. A century ago it was topical and related to the playhouses which drew large audiences; its equivalent in terms of present-day public entertainment is the tiny screen designed as a toy television set which utilises an optical illusion device of silhouetted cartoon and black-and-white bars to give an effect of animation. But the spoken lines identified with the toy-theatre characters seem to have disappeared entirely from the many new variants of animated book-toys which have, in a feeble way, attempted to replace them.

Only a small proportion of those who live in London realise that in about forty minutes, by Underground from Charing Cross, one can be in the middle of the largest toy-making estate in the whole world. When, long ago, the arrival in our street of a scooter, or, on the occasion of the world-shaking birthday when one's grandfather's gift was a magnificent toy called a "Fairy Cycle," one little imagined that a day would come when one would be discussing toy-history with the man who invented, marketed, and won international fame for these and scores of other British toys.

107. An early example of a Benjamin Pollock toy theatre (*c.* 1860) with stage fully set

Mr. Walter Lines, veteran industrialist and one of England's toy-pioneers, hailing from what he described as the "backwoods days of toy-making," told me that his father used to take him along with him to the traders at the Lowther Arcade. He remembered talking to William Whiteley at Westbourne Grove; to Gordon Selfridge, "the man who fundamentally changed retailing," in his top-room in West London, where they discussed the latest gadget across a colossal desk flanked by a massive fireplace. More exciting than all this—he it was who "personally carried out the orders for the Queen of Spain's dolls' house, complete with baths, flush-toilets, electricity —all the newest devices, just before the combustion-engine had been invented." He made the fabulous baby-carriage for the Sultan of Zanzibar, and splendid rocking-horses for royal chldren everywhere.

Holder of the Royal Warrant since 1760, his organisation speaks proudly of "the finest toyshop in the world," a claim made with justification, since the six-floor store in London's famous Regent Street, when decorated and illuminated for Christmas buyers, is one of the memorable sights of a Metropolis in fective mood.

At the Merton works one assimilates such statistical data as that the factories put approximately fifty million wheels a year on to wheel-toys that roll into most countries of the world; that it would have taken one four hours to do a complete tour of the twenty-five-acre plant; that eight thousand employees here at bench and lathe, press and drill, fashion and box toys whose trademarks have put England into the very front line of toy-design and toy-making today. More thrilling in one way was my meeting with craftsmen like Herbert Staines and Charles Rathbone, men who have been making rocking-horses by hand for generations. In the chapters on *Toys That Move* is recounted something of these men's story; how they might be seen lovingly handling the ancient wheelwright's tool known as the spoke-shovel, and working with the draw-knife and the chopper.

This merchant prince of British toy-making, the man who closely watched and lived through the hegemony and collapse, the revival and reorganisation of England's deadliest rival in the industry, and perhaps knowing more about the details of toy-marketing than any other Englishman, provided a link with this ancient wood-carving craft, and its fine old artisans. Some of them, over eighty years old, he had employed in the Islington and Tottenham toy-factories years previously.

Many remarkable gaps would be filled in our knowledge if a

108. Victorian butcher's shop, *c.* 1850. Each of the realistically coloured joints is removable

109. West's Toy Theatre Establishment in Exeter Street, Strand, 1812

definitive story of the British Toy Industry were compiled. Indeed, it is the memoirs of such dynamic participants as Walter Lines which would provide much of the laughter and tears in its unfolding. A strong impression which one takes away from a tour of this empire of toy-manufacture is that teachers and pupils alike, if permitted, could derive more value and stimulus from one hours's visit to its doll-making shops, or the buildings where Triang steel toys are produced, than from many a classroom period on theoretical aspects of history and geography, science and economics.

The progression from the Dickensian shop, with its penny toys and diamond-shaped panes, to the Victorian arcade was as great a stride as the modern Toy Fair at Leipzig or Harrogate is an advance on the market-square of the Middle Ages. The Toy Emporium is a feature of our times. And, although during the war years Father Christmas was virtually asked, "Is Your Journey Really Necessary?" he has now happily been reinstated to his important function within the national life. As presiding genius of the annual toy-town pageant, he has resumed his role of shaking thousands of small hands amid lavish scenes sometimes devised on a Technicolor scale of grandeur. Leading department stores seek to out-rival each other in dramatising Santa Claus and his ceremonies. The spirit of Peter Pan is always with us, and a recent Christmas Season found the larger stores in competition with each other catering for the great festival of toy-gifts. Small visitors had a choice of meeting Father Christmas in person, by devious means of travel. They could either board the Good Ship *Jolly Roger* for Never-Never-Land; they could switchback over the Alps, riding a sleigh to Jingle Town. Alternatively, they might journey through an enchanted forest to the Pixies' Workshop, or through Alice-in-Wonderland Glade to meet the scarlet-robed Saint, in the company of his newest vicar on earth—a genial and corpulent gent sporting mutton-chop whiskers, a sort of half John Bull, half Uncle Sam, and christened Uncle Holly, though the latter name would have meant precious little to our parents.

Equalled only by a visit to Pantomime and the Circus is the annual pilgrimage to the Toyland Bazaar, for where else can one find such a concentration of fairy lights and spangles; of cotton-wool snow and shimmering tinsel, laughter and wonderment, as at these wonderlands of colour and wide eyes?

The selling of toys employs its own publicity methods. That these were just as bold and original in the nineteenth century is witnessed by an old handbill, an amusing example of how a toy-merchant, one Pierotti, advertised his merchandise in rhyme (110). The document is so intriguing that I pursued my research until its story came to light, aided jointly by Mr. Gibbs-Smith, of the Victoria and Albert Museum, and Mr. Goddard Watts, who is a great-grandson of the toy-merchant Pierotti.

Mr. Watts revealed that the London Crystal Palace as printed on the sheet was *not* the famous Exhibition Hall, but was the name given to a toy and fancy goods shop in Oxford Street. It was there that his great-grandfather rented the gallery for his dolls. This show continued in Hamley's premises, and the family association with Hamley's continued until a few years before the last war.

The Pierotti family, it appears, had been making dolls in this country probably since 1720, when the original Pierotti came over from Italy "after having fallen out of an apple tree and fractured his skull." He came to have his injury seen to at St. Bartholomew's Hospital, and had such a terrible journey to England that he never went back but took up residence in London and sold toys for a living. In Italy the Pierotti family had apparently been doll-makers continuously from about 1100.

Mr. Gibbs-Smith, upon checking records of the 1851 loan exhibits, found that the museum had a number of offers of objects allegedly bought "at the Crystal Palace," including dolls, a speciality of Pierotti. He finally established that the firm in fact did not exhibit anything in the Great Exhibition of 1851, but had given their gallery the title *London Crystal Palace*.

"Your handbill," as he wrote to Mr. Goddard Watts, "finally clears up the doubt as to why these offers are made to me, because quite obviously they derive from grandmothers and great-grandmothers who visited the Pierotti shop, and who told their relatives that the objects were bought 'in the Crystal Palace,' which strictly speaking was quite true!"

In contrast to the plebeian booths and toy-counters in the street-markets, a more elegant atmosphere obtains in the glass-covered-in shopping centre which adjoins Piccadilly and Savile Row, the Burlington Arcade. Here, at the celebrated Number Fifty, H.M. Queen Mary was a frequent visitor in search of new miniature furnishings for her famous dolls' house. Here, too, the then Prince of Wales would regularly come to buy toys for the young Princesses. Other royal shoppers included the Duchess of Kent and the Duchess of Gloucester, whose last visit to this old-fashioned and picturesque toyshop, the

H. PIEROTTI,

GALLERY, LONDON CRYSTAL PALACE,

OXFORD STREET.

H. PIEROTTI respectfully informs his Patrons and the Public he has considerably ENLARGED HIS STOCK, to which he has added NEW STOCK, in which will be found an extensive Assortment of French and German Toys, Mediæval Articles, Work Boxes, Rosewood Writing Desks, Dressing Cases, &c., &c.

My Juvenile Friends who to the Crystal Palace come,
And require a Sword, Violin, Trumpet or Drum,
A Shovel, a Barrow, a Rake, or a Spade,
You'll find at our Counter the best that are made :
The New Eagle Kite, with Traps, Balls, and Bats,
German Boxes of Toys, and Musical Cats,
The **GAME** of **AUNT SALLY**, an English Farm,
And Pop-guns from France that will do you no harm ;
To keep you in health, 'tis my wish to contrive,
With the New Royal Game, that's called **JACK'S ALIVE**.
Such beautiful Dolls that will open their Eyes,
You may wash, comb and dress them, and not fear their cries ;
The Game of " *La Grace*," Skipping Ropes, Plates and Dishes,
Battledores, Shuttlecocks, and Magnetic Fishes,
There's Little Black Topsy, and Poor Uncle Tom !
A large Rocking Horse which you may ride on,
And at the Year's end my young friends to please,
A profusion of Goods for the famed **Christmas Trees**.
So dear little friends, just bear this in mind,
'Tis at **H. PIEROTTI'S** these wonders you'll find.

GAMES of the RACE, REGATTA & STAG HUNT.

Observe the Address—

H. PIEROTTI, Inventor of the Royal Model Dolls,

Gallery, London Crystal Palace, Oxford Street.

110. Handbill published by H. Pierotti, nineteenth century

delight of so many children young and old, took place at Christmas, 1950. "Last visit" has a melancholy ring, but in the opinion of its retired owner, Mr. Eric C. Morel, it is apt, because the business which his grandfather established in the London of 1820 was closed down in the autumn of 1951. Going back there one day, to talk about its history with "the toy-man Morel," and finding a blank where had always stood a gay and happy landmark in the West End, evoked something of the quality of a bad dream, like visiting a wood that has been charred, of finding a birds' nest filled with snow, lonely and deserted.

When its founder decided to trade in toys he specialised in the most artistic designs, but also carried the usual stocks of trains, dolls, teddy bears and so on. A taste for the fine arts led him to concentrate on ivory, silver, and wooden miniatures; diminutive pieces dear to the small child's heart—dolls' house furniture, delicately wrought; period toys; rare little items in Bohemian glass. Visitors came from all over the world to see and purchase Morel's famous historical figures, correctly dressed in every detail; knights-in-armour in their movable visors with splendidly emblazoned shields; soldiers in the uniforms of many periods, and armies which attracted collectors from overseas, who had learned of Morel's from the intelligence of the collectors' brotherhood and who, by correspondence, had remained his devout patrons.

When, during the last war, it was found quite impossible to put on sale goods which lived up to a reputation for being out-of-the-ordinary, the firm diligently sought, and was lucky to find, a number of artists who could make superb miniatures by hand. Now, sad to relate, all these craftsmen have passed away, a tragedy of our times; and, with their passing, they have finally closed a door and a chapter separating the nineteenth century, with its fondness for the quaint and the finely wrought, from our plastic age, wherein appearance often counts for more than artistry and the individualistic personal note.[1]

At the time of the Great Exhibition of 1851 there flourished, on the north side of the Strand, the famous Lowther Arcade, a place of pilgrimage for children. As admission was free, and the place was regarded as one of the sights of London, it was continually thronged with children and their attendants buying toys. Many of the shops in

---

[1] Noteworthy modern artists who have created toys include Edith Reynolds of London; Edward Andrews of Yarmouth and Alan Smith of Kingswear, Devon.

the Arcade were Swiss, French and German, so that the toys offered were of a wide variety and assortment, including many from Japan and China. In all probability many of the items now finding their way to different English toy collections were originally purchased here.

Edward Walford describes the Arcade in his book *London Old and New.* "Nearly opposite the railway station," he records, "and running diagonally towards Adelaide Street, was the Arcade. Nearly 200 feet in length, it has shops on either side for the sale of fancy goods." The atmosphere of this bazaar, to which the juvenile population of the country were drawn as by a magnet, can be fully recaptured by the painstaking water-colours executed about 1801 by the German artist Scharff, now in the Prints Department of the British Museum. In these meticulous sketches of the Strand shops, Scharff has drawn the name and trade of each owner together with the signboards and other distinctive shop-front features—thereby providing us with a vivid documentary impression of the atmosphere of the contemporary scene.

VIII

THE TOY IN MUSIC, IN BOOKS AND AT EASTER

1. TOYS IN MUSIC

PERHAPS the most evocative association with the Lowther Arcade, as with so much of Victorian London, is through popular music. One of the most typical songs of those days is Fred Cape's charming composition *The Lowther Arcade*, sometimes known as *The Tin Gee-Gee*—a number which was a special favourite at the old Gaiety Music Hall. Many people today remember this melody, if not the words, from having heard it sung by an older generation. The first occasion that I heard *The Tin Gee-Gee* sung was at the close of the last year, at the Players Theatre in Albemarle Street. There, "every night except Sunday," Ridgeway's Late Joys delighted members who heard, re-invoked in this ditty full of innocent pathos, the elusive magic of the Arcade. Moreover, it is pleasant to think that even today those who seek something of the spirit of Queen Victoria's reign may listen to the inimitable Archie Harradine singing about the Saucy Little Doll and love-lorn Toy Cavalryman at the period theatre in Villiers Street, a building which stands on the site where Gatti's boisterous Under-the-Arches Music Hall once stood.

Such themes and threads of music woven into childhood are as an epiphany. As we grow older, we come to distinguish the separate strands, and begin to value their associations and meaning.

The Little Toy Soldier, as rendered by John McCormack's tenor voice, is for me a tune to be remembered for ever. Its power inspired a dialogue phantasy what happened when the dust-laden soldiers of France, Germany and Britain woke up in the toy-cupboard, fifty years after "Boy Blue had put them there." Its appeal led me on to discover the now almost forgotten character of Eugene Field, its American composer, a personality of curious and naïve grandeur.

It is not widely known outside the United States that the author of *The Little Toy Soldier* also wrote *Love Songs of Childhood* and *With Trumpet and Drum*, two volumes containing some of the sweetest child verse of those times.

Eugene Field had a magical room, where Santa Claus, the Good Fairy Godmother, Fairy Land and the Land of Nod are real persons and places. He more than half believed in Witches and Hobgoblins, and to the end of his life he was afraid to enter a dark room alone. Rarely did he enjoy being left to himself; and to the day of his death he had the heart and impulses of a boy, loving animals, gorgeous colours, perfumes and mechanical toys which go with a clicketty noise. In a sense, his home was a small toyshop, with items of all kinds and descriptions, but he loved the mechanical toys the best.

Every Saturday morning he went home laden with toys not only for his own two children, Roswell and Ruth, but for a number of young friends who lived in Chicago.

He bought dolls by the dozen for the girls, and his own little boy had more elephants than were ever shot by African travellers. Shortly before he died, Eugene Field bought a big elephant and a big brown bear for "Posey," his nickname for Roswell. Every time anyone called (it made no difference who it was), the elephant and the big brown bear were wound up, and away they would go, their heads nodding back and forth as if they were alive.

Every schoolchild learning to play the piano must at some stage have fled from the tedium of scale-practice into the escape-world of toys. It is remarkable to what extent the animated toy has attracted composers. It still exerts the same fascination on the musical mind which puppets, mechanical dolls, tumblers and marionettes have kindled in the imaginations of musicians like Tchaikowsky, Gounod and Debussy. The creation of such ballets as *Boutique fantasque*, *The Sleeping Princess* or *Mother Goose Suite* are directly inspired by the toy idea.

What would the Christmas pantomime be without a toyland ballet of some kind ? Toys which come to life on the stage hold, for children, a degree of wonder and the mystery of poetry and movement. One of the most enjoyable performances given in this genre was the ballet-sequence in the London Palladium's *Babes in the Wood*, in which Pauline Grant was choreographer and St. John Roper and Daphne Lee designed the superb costumes and masks.

2. THE TOY IN BOOKS FOR CHILDREN

Gröber in his studies mentions that "the attempt to give the semblance of life to artificial figures is as old as the hills." The animated toy invested with movement very soon finds its way into the realms of fiction and fantasy, for flights of fancy to which composers of music were moved by such an idea are achieved by the writers of prose.

The art of story-telling, from Aesop to A. A. Milne, is heightened by examples of the toy brought to life. The Banbury Chap Books and Nursery Toy Book literature are full of references to such characteristic juvenile productions as *The Adventures of a Whizzing Top*. Many were illustrated by Rusher's famous cuts. Children's librarians hold the view that the adventures of Hans Andersen's Tin Soldier ought to be as much an integral part of a child's reading as the antics of Mickey Mouse or Muffin the Mule.

Most Victorian story-books had a lightly handled content which contrasted with the usual underlying didactic purpose. This is how the anonymous author of *Memoirs of the Lady Seraphina* prefaces her dramatisation of a doll's adventures:

"My principal intention, or rather aim, in writing this little book, was to amuse children by a story founded on one of their favourite diversions, and to inculcate a few such minor morals as my little plot might be strong enough to carry; chiefly the domestic happiness produced by kind temper and consideration for others. And further, I wished to say a word in favour of that good old-fashioned plaything, the Doll, which one now sometimes hears decried by sensible people who have no children of their own."

Seraphina, a wax doll, perched on a shelf in the bazaar, overhears two schoolboys trying to decide how they can spend their last sixpence. A gentleman gives them good advice, suggesting that they buy "something useful" and not squander their pennies on cakes. The doll is puzzled:

"One word used by the gentleman made a great impression on me—'useful.' What could that mean? Various considerations were suggested by the question. Some things, it seemed, were useful, others not; and what puzzled me most was, that the very same things appeared to be useful to some people, and not to others. For instance, the sixpenny paint-box, which had been rejected as useless to Willy, was bought soon afterwards by a small boy, who said it would be the most useful toy he had. Could this be the case with everything?"

The story proceeds to the irrevocable moment when the doll's fate is decided and she passes the boundaries of the world of toys and enters a new state of existence "in my little mistress's hands." The story ends in autobiographical vein, which is charming without being sentimental:

"As we turned to leave the room, Susan and her little sister lingered for a moment behind the others, and the child held me up towards Rose. Rose started, and exclaimed: 'Is it possible? It really *is* my poor old Seraphina. Who would have thought of her being still in existence? What a good, useful doll she has been! I really must give her a kiss once more for old friendship's sake.' So saying, she kissed both me and the baby, and we left the house.

"And now there remains but little more for me to relate. My history and my existence are fast drawing to an end; my last wish has been gratified by my meeting with Rose, and my first hope realised by her praise of my usefulness. She has since given the baby a new doll, and I am finally laid on the shelf, to enjoy, in company with my respected friend the Pen, a tranquil old age. When he, like myself, was released from active work, and replaced by one of Mordan's patent steel, he kindly offered to employ his remaining leisure in writing from my dictation, and it is in compliance with his advice that I have thus ventured to record my experience."

This treatment still perseveres in English oral juvenile literature. Yet very few authors have an intrinsic feeling for the toy, and the quality of the true fairy-tale often eludes attempts at personification. Successful stories of the present century in this genre are *The Wonderful Journey* and the *Strange Adventures of a Toy Soldier* by C. W. Beaumont.

The former is a dream-sequence in which the boy hero is carried high over the clouds on his rocking-horse magnificently come to life. In the second, no less fantastic, the adventures are conceived from the perspective of the little soldier himself. It is not always that an illustrator interprets so warmly a story-teller's ideas as Wyndham Payne has done in both these stories.

It is strange how, in the cavalcade of toys, the soldier seems to be the foremost character in the animated story. He moves through history, depicted as the rigid wooden Hussar, but unchanged in his appearance though armaments and equipments may alter. Historically interesting is a book for children entitled *Toyland in the Air*, on account of the amusing drawings which fix the story so very definitely at the period of the 1914-1918 war, when balloons and dirigibles formed a common image in the popular mind.

The use of toys to illustrate AEC Books is a rewarding study. Examples reveal how the subject matter has changed little during three hundred years, although the design and function of toys have gone through minor changes. It was an arduous task wandering through London's streets trying to find appropriate toys with the initial letter of the alphabet which Cyril Beaumont and Eileen Mayo finally achieved in the publication of *Toys*.

3. TOY BOOK OR BOOK-TOY?

Once an esoteric hobby, the collecting of old Chap Books, Horn Books, Nursery Rhyme editions, Primers and kindred publications has assumed proportions which are a reflection of the growing interest that the layman is taking in Nursery Toy Book literature for its own sake.[1]

If the adjectival use of "book" is correct, these early contrivances, which were aimed at stimulating an interest in things extraneous to the child's experience through play, strictly speaking, ought to have been named Book-Toys instead of Toy Books.

The general trend from the toy-that-was-a-book to the book that is intrinsically a toy is characteristic of our times. *Mother Goose's Nursery Rhymes*, which was, until the turn of the century, a mere collection of traditional verses and popular illustrations, is now obtainable in forms ranging from novelty cut-outs and manipulatory effects in the pages to toy theatres or peepshow devices. These offer to children more scope for dramatising the stories in their own fashion through physical use of the book itself, and employing ingenious systems of animation induced through paper levers and tabs.

Only a few years after the end of the war there came back on the market elaborate old and new kinds of cut-out-story-books, the latest innovation being an original type in which the paper models for a circus are pre-cut on the page—no scissors, no paste required!

Another welcome revival among cut-out book-toys is the *Peepshow* series. By turning back the covers the six scenes are made to open out like a fan, each one representing the Sleeping Beauty, Puss in Boots, Cinderella, Ali Baba or the Three Bears.

Once a toy has become, in a manner of speaking, "part of the national life," it finds its way on to greeting cards, novelties, postcards with moving tabs, and as replicas of branded products for playing games of shop.

4. THE TOY AT EASTER

Within the juvenile almanac Easter novelties and toys play their recognised seasonal role. Just like the stocking at Christmas or

---

[1] E. S. Taylor, *History of Playing Cards*; Andrew Tuer, *History of The Horn Book*; Gumuchian, *Les Livres de l'enfance du XV au XIX Siècle*; F. V. Barry, *A Century of Children's Books* (Chap Books and Ballads).

the pancakes at Shrovetide, these objects perpetuate traditional customs in the Christian year.

Though the toys themselves are a comparatively recent innovation, the two basic ideas from which they derive are older than Christianity. One is the chicken; the other is the Easter rabbit. Both are ancient symbols of fertility, and, through different mythological links, are identified with the egg.

The egg, in some religious beliefs of the East, was associated mystically with the idea of eternity. Egg-eating, as a cult, was a relic of the "mundane egg," an object for which, according to ancient Persian wisdom, Ormuzd and Ahriman were obliged to contend "till the consummation of all things." We have evidence, also, that the Chinese, about nine hundred years before Christ, used to offer eggs during a festival held in the spring of their year. These were thanksgiving offerings to the gods who had caused the storms to abate and the floods to subside in the rivers, and so permitted an agrarian community to proceed with the task of growing its food.

To commemorate the deliverance of the Israelites from Pharaoh's hosts, when the Angel of Death passed over their tents but smote the Egyptian first-born, Jews to this day who partake of the Passover supper include eggs as a special dish. These are usually hard-boiled, shelled and served whole in a gravy made from salt and plain water. The Passover eggs are intended to represent both the spirit of thanksgiving and the pious remembrance of past miracles.

With a long history and universal usage behind it, the egg accordingly became a very natural choice for the early Christians, who wished to symbolise Jesus rising from the tomb. The fish had already become an emblem for their faith, and it is of interest to find that in France to this day it is the hollow fish (made in chocolate or cardboard), and not the hollow egg, in which children are presented with their Easter trinkets. Known there as *poisson d'Avril*, it has a dual association with All Fools' Day and the traditional French notion that everybody ate mackerels or herrings on April 1.

To the early believers in the Resurrection, living close to the earth, acquainted with simple parable and analogy's power, the chick entombed in its shell, breaking out into the light every Eastertide with regenerate life, became the obvious symbol for the Christian message.

As time passed the Medieval Church looked upon eggs as holy gifts. Then the devout used to offer them to their priests. The next stage was for them to be brought into the Church, where they were used in the ritual. The custom of blessing the eggs on Easter Saturday morning is still observed in Mediterranean countries, notably Italy and Cyprus. The parish priest visits those homes where the table is laid out with special Easter sweetmeats. After the blessing, the members of the household, especially the eager-eyed children, may eat the egg dishes. In Russia, where the Orthodox rite was followed, the giving of hand-painted eggs in baskets is a time-old tradition. The peasants in the nineteenth century perfected a series of wooden eggs for children, each one enclosing a size still smaller. Among the aristocracy the fashion developed for commissioning jewellers to make sumptuous eggs from precious metals. This art reached a high peak in the workmanship of the great artist-goldsmith Fabergé,[1] who fashioned rare examples, some from solid gold inlaid with pearls, for the Tzar and his entourage.

In England, after the Reformation eggs were excluded from all Church ceremonies. Like many another ritual discarded by adults, these egg customs were taken over entirely by children's play-patterns. About fifty years ago egg games were commonly played at Easter. Today even in rural England they are dying out. In a few undisturbed communities eggs are rolled down a grassy slope on Easter Monday by children who try to race them to the bottom. In this form the play is held to commemorate the rolling away of the stone from the tomb of the risen Christ.

In Preston, Lancashire, boys still "go pace-egging" at Easter.[2] The pace-egg (which is an English version of *Pash* Egg or *Pasch* Egg) was simply a hard-boiled egg with its shell coloured or painted. In Westmorland, where the folk-game survives, the lads are known as jollyboys and visit local houses on Easter Monday where they enact an ancient play similar in style and content to the mummer plays recited by the Wren boys on St. Stephen's Day.[3] As soon as the door of the visited home is opened, the jollyboys walk round in a circle, singing the rhyme by which the drama is introduced:

> "Now we're jolly pace-eggers all in one round
> We've come a pace-egging, we hope you'll prove kind:
> We hope you'll prove kind with your eggs and strong beer,
> For we'll come no more near you until the next year.
> Fol de diddle ol, fol de dee, dol de diddle ol dum day."

[1] H. C. Bainbridge, *Peter Carl Fabergé*.
[2] J. Harland, *Legends and Traditions of Lancashire*, p. 101.
[3] M. Danielli, *Folk-Lore*, Vol. LXIII, December, 1951.

The dyeing of pace-eggs in such country districts where the practice is still followed is done by wrapping the eggs in onion skins. An attractive brown and pale mottled effect is obtained by cutting the onion skins into patterns and sticking these to the shells before boiling. The peasants of the Slav countries have developed this form of shell-decoration into a fine art, and children are taught at school how to create Easter novelties based on the egg theme. Polish peasants use hay and red beetroot or cabbage as an alternative to onion for dyes. They mark off with liquid wax the patterns on the shell not to be coloured. They then dye the eggs in the various solutions. The results are very lovely to look at, and children at school are taught to create Easter-toys based on the decorated *motifs*. In Czechoslovakia the boys call on the girls' homes, where they chant such jingles as: "If you don't give me an egg I shall most certainly be spanked." In Sweden verses pointing out each family-member's foibles are scribbled on the eggs before they are served at breakfast. French children keep their eggs and use them to try to win more from their playmates in a kind of marble game. In parts of Holland, like Gelderland and Overyssel, children march along the streets in groups, carrying a stick pleasantly designed as a tree, on the top of which is placed a cock made of baked flour. They call the tree *Palm Paschen*.

Baked dough, intended originally to be shaped like a Pascal lamb, is the Spanish tradition. The amateur pastry-cooks are, however, so unskilled that the lamb usually turns out to resemble a monkey. *Mona de Pascua* (Easter she-monkey) is the name in Spanish given to the cakes thus made and richly filled with almonds, candied fruit and decorated with eggs. The colours of the eggs have vital significance. For a sweetheart the egg must be pink. For a mother-in-law it must be yellow. An egg painted black means trouble in store for its donor. Naturally, children who give or receive these Easter tokens take care not to get the colours confused.

The confectioned egg is a newcomer to England. It was first introduced by Dutch and French confectioners about 1900. Until then the making of chocolate eggs was a complicated operation, slow and very expensive. They were made from tinplate moulds by hand, in two separate halves, and trimmed. Later, mechanical processes made it possible to produce hundreds in the time formerly needed to make one. The first examples were enormous shells of smooth chocolate, expensively beribboned and decorated with edible flowers in coloured sugar. Then followed smaller solid eggs made of marzipan with pink icing twirlingly piped along the seam. These were sometimes embellished with a coloured scrap or picture of an Easter chick or Easter bunny. Other varieties of solid milk chocolate, the size of hen-eggs, were wrapped in gay foils, purple, emerald, gold and crimson, their whites made from marshmallow filling, their yolks of sweet creams, packed in baskets and cushioned in nests of coloured-paper straw. Others were cunningly contrived from sugar to resemble the spotted eggs of birds laid in nests of chocolate. Edible eggs today range from coated jelly to disguised toffee. Non-edible eggs were first manufactured of pasteboard and were extremely large—almost too huge for a child to handle is the impression gained from a French illustration of a nursery scene in 1880, captioned *Œufs de Pâques*, in which the small child is depicted struggling to separate the two halves. The mass production of pasteboard shells, brightly designed with chickens, hares and rabbits, was carried on in Germany and sold in large numbers in England. To pasteboard as a material have been added tin, wood, plaster, Bohemian crystal, cellulose or coloured plastic. Victorian children prized eggs which were covered in velvet cloth, with borders of paper lace, keeping them from season to season.

The English Easter-bunny toy has its origin in the Germanic legend of the Easter Hare, or *Der Oster Hase*. In Austria it is invariably a white hare who comes faithfully every Easter to deposit sugar eggs and sweets in the moss nests which children carefully prepare for him, placing these in gardens on Good Friday. The association of eggs and hares' nests is believed to originate in the habits of broody hens looking for a ready-made nest in which to secretly hatch their eggs. The finding of a hare's form close at hand was an obvious nesting-site, and so country children romping through the fields would accidentally come upon the hares' nests with eggs in them, and assume naturally, in their innocence, that the long-eared animal had left them there. So powerful would seem to be the appeal of this myth from the Teutonic countries that English story-books for children at the beginning of the twentieth century take the legend for granted and perpetuate it by appropriate drawings and verses. The following lines, typical of the children's books of 1895, suggest a possible direct translation from the German:

> "What is that in the grass out there?
> Look, oh, look, a hare, a hare!
> Peeping out, the long-eared puss,
> From his cosy nest at us.

There he goes, away, away,
Over earth and stones and clay.
Quick, you children, come and see
This glorious nest for you and me.
The prettiest thing you ever saw,
Grass and hay and moss and straw.
Look inside, what have we found?
Coloured eggs so smooth and round.
See them lie each by his fellow,
Blue and green and red and yellow.
Little hare in yonder wood,
Thank you, thank you, kind and good."

One of the most elaborate constructions designed as an Easter toy is in the Percy Muir Collection. It is shaped faithfully like an egg, about twelve inches long and eight inches high, and covered with rich red plush. At the base is a musical movement which is wound by a key. When the spring is fully wound a tune is played and suddenly, following a few bars, the upper lid of the shell springs upwards like the lid of a Jack-in-the-box. After another few notes of the melody out pops the head of a white rabbit, covered in real fur, and with pink glass eyes. The effect is grotesque and likely to fill the average child with apprehension. Yet the toy is typical of something produced at the whim of a wealthy patron determined to have the most extravagant Easter egg that money and the latest mechanical devices could secure.

IX

HISTORICAL RETROSPECT

IN a survey of toys from ancient times to the present day the general impression is that in shape and design they are as varied as the stones of the seashore or the flowers of the field. Superficially this seems to be true enough. Yet what emerges from a close examination of their history is that these thousands of forms and varieties, which seem to be endless, all emanate from a very few archetypal patterns.

To penetrate through the superstructures of refinement and elaboration and to find these basic patterns, we must revert to the religious objects which many authorities persist in calling "prehistoric toys." Such material, concentrated in the museums of Germany, Czechoslovakia and Russia, and dating from the period between the Bronze and the Iron Age in Europe, should be examined in the light of pre-Egyptian finds prior to Mesopotamian civilisations, such as were recently excavated in the sub-continent of India. Such correlation would give fruitful results in establishing whether in fact the archetypal patterns are not more than two thousand years before the Christian Era, or go back to the very dawn of man's consciousness.

Archetype Number One is globular. It is the shape of a fruit, a large nut or gourd. Hollowed out, with seeds dried inside to make a noise, these were the very first rattles. It cannot be proved that they were used for infantile pleasure, but they certainly were the objects from which the modern baby-rattle derived. The examples preserved are of baked clay or pottery. The dominant shape is spherical, but variants shaped as eggs, kegs, bulbous vases with short necks show how more complex artistic ideas began to emerge from the circular rattle.

These noise-makers were essentially ritualistic apparatus. Together with clapper-wheels, corn-crakes and bull-roarers they had a social and religious value far more serious than the mere amusement of children. A bull-roarer, for instance, was used to invoke the rain-god by the Egyptian field-worker. It was a piece of wood attached to a string which, on being whirled round rapidly, produced a loud rumbling sound. With bull-roarers in hand they believed that the rumbling would be answered by the claps of thunder and that the god would send them water from the skies. In primitive communities this device is still used in its magico-religious role, *i.e.* to frighten away evil spirits.[1]

The spherical shape gave us the ball, and all manner of rolling objects used in ball-games. Cut in half, it gave us the rocker, used as a basis for both the weighted tumbler and the set of wooden bowls (half eggs) peculiar to Russian toy-design.

Archetype Number Two would appear to be the bird-shape. Fundamentally it is the egg-shape of Number One with a beaked head and a plumed tail appended. This bird-image is first found in prehistoric clay whistles, objects which also had a sacred significance in hunting or sacrifice. The early ones, found in Rome *c.* 200 B.C., were of baked clay. Down the centuries the pattern has changed little from the glazed ceramic hen-whistles of the sixteenth and seventeenth centuries to the distinctive form of Slavonic wooden folk-toy exemplifying farmyard fowl and pet birds of every conceivable kind, to the English penny-toys celebrated in Gordon Craig's album, or the whistling cock-a-doodle-doo in plastic or tin which is a popular noise-maker of today.

Remarkable is the preponderance of bird-images which haunted the makers of the early mechanical toys. With so many floral, animal or human shapes to choose from, their imaginations were attracted by the primeval force which the bird-image exerted on their imagination.

All these bird-types, whether clay peacock, fluffy chicken, lacquered never-never-bird or wooden rooster, have a common ancestor in the bird-whistles of antiquity.

Some of the rattles already mentioned were made in the shape of pigeons, fantails and cockerels. Rarely were the heads of quadrupeds affixed to rattles. The few which have been discovered seem to resemble a long-eared animal like a rabbit, but the body and base are still concealed in the ball-shape, there being no legs in evidence.

The characteristic of four legs classifies the varieties originating from Archetype Number Three. This may be described as the standing animal, from which all rigid animal toys have evolved. The first known example is in the form of a horse, primitive, elemental, riderless: four legs, a body, neck and tail. From this unmounted archetype has grown every kind of four-legged toy animal: the painted wooden cows of Egyptians; the tiger with movable jaws;

[1] Best, *Games and Pastimes of the Maori,* and Haddon, *Study of Man.*

the ichneumon with snake; the wooden animals in farmyard or stable sets; the Noah's Ark menagerie; all the four-legged species and sub-species which form a Darwinian cavalcade linking the rocking-horse and the cuddly soft animals with those ill-proportioned stationary Greek and Roman horses of painted day.

Investing animals with movement is simply a secondary process, a later addition to the basic shape. Therefore, by genealogical deduction, such animals-with-movement toys as the monkey-up-a-stick or the peasant-and-the-bear all derive from the archetypal quadruped.

Archetype Number Four is the mounted rider. In this pattern we note the combination of four-legged quadruped and human figurine. In the duality we see a road where two distinct directions fork. The first is the horse intended to be moved about in a war-game, progenitor of the mounted cavalryman. Placed on wheels—according on the Chandarro (Indian) and Susa (Persian) specimens—these became the ancestral pattern of the toy-on-wheels, whether pushed or pulled, or graduating into an automaton with special attributes.

The oldest pull-toy is in the form of horse-and-wagon, wheel-mounted. It comes from the early charioteer, a replica in which the vehicles and the warrior are complementary.

The divergent concept in Archetype Number Four is the human figurine. This is like a bridge spanning the gap between Number Four and the final key-pattern, Archetype Number Five.

From the reproduction of the human figure, erect, two-armed and two-legged, we can visualise the growth in its many manifestations of the female prototype—the doll. Side by side with that growth we can trace the continuity of the man-toy. Whether in the form of string-puppet or jumping-jack, clockwork clown or simian actor, trick cyclist or money-eating saving-box, these hundreds of variations may be shown to be on the common theme of man.

With five such patriarchal sources to guide us, we can the more easily appreciate the aesthetic and metaphysical factors which have influenced the evolution of the toy. The terms of reference are as valid for the cultures of the Nile Valley as for the Roman system which was pushed northwards through Gaul into the Celtic and Saxon societies of the British Isles. We have evidence in what the Romans brought to England from Italy and Gaul that though the clay was local, the cunning in fashioning it was Italian.[1]

Although study of the Gaelic regions furnishes us with proof that

[1] Roman Clay Toys, Colchester Museum.

table-games were played by the Celts, and that such playthings as jackstones, dice, sticks and stones were used in their games of skill, there is a gap in our knowledge of toys in respect of the Saxon world. One commentator has remarked that "no doubt the existence of Saxon children presumes the existence of Saxon toys," but it is only now that research is taking the trouble to investigate a problem long neglected by students of pre-Norman England.

With the Normans, as we have seen, came French influence—a combining of games necessary to keep the youth valiant and aware of its superiority with an art of gamesmanship which was taught according to fixed codes and etiquette that were respected by all. As Norman-French and Anglo-Saxon mingled to form the bedrock of British civilisation, a race was produced of seafaring men who voyaged to many lands and brought back from abroad ideas and devices which, in turn, became a part of the English pattern of toys and play.

From the fourteenth century onwards toys in England reflect closely nearly every characteristic of Western European discoveries, development and innovations. There was a two-way traffic after the nineteenth century, when German and French leadership in toy manufacture presented a strong challenge to British industrial supremacy.

Till then, as a result of free trade and of her role as a great mercantile nation, into England came toys of all kinds, and nationalities. They duly helped to entertain and influence English children down the years. They enriched childhood in ways not easy to dissect. Conversely, they exported from England mannerisms and rules of play in the English language to America, Canada, Australia, New Zealand and many other countries, where people learned to use the words *bat* and *ball*, *soldier* and *doll*, or the inexplicably more evocative names like snakes-and-ladders, shuttlecock or tiddlywinks, which contain a linguistic ethos all their own, and which, like the things children say to their toys, are quite untranslatable.

Appendix

SOME TOY COLLECTIONS

Toys are miniatures, microcosms. They reproduce in little the adult contemporary world. They image man and all his surroundings, his weapons, houses, machines, tools, and even his won toys, the paraphernalia of sport.[1]

A FIRST visit to see Miss Joyce Holt's collection of toys (95) at her lakeside home in Kendal is an unforgettable experience. Her idea in starting such a hobby really began in childhood when she and her sister had their curiosity and appetite whetted by a reference in one of Gertrude Jekyll's Garden Books mentioning that she had a toy-cupboard. Miss Holt and her playmate would not rest until they had something similar. "To cut a long story short," she observes, "we had a valuable Adam dinner-service hanked out of the cabinet which had been made specially to house it. Immediately the toys seemed to take possession and they have occupied this piece of furniture ever since."

The glass showcase was filled from enthusiasm, and with no definite thought of making a famous collection; still less with the idea that one day "it would become important enough to be included and photographed in a book on the subject. We started the hobby simply because we were enthralled by toys, for their own sake and for what they offered to our maturing imaginations."

The collection falls into two groups. The first is in a small corner-cupboard devoted to precious miniatures in all kinds of material, trinkets, carved cherry-stones, charms and dolls' pieces. This, situated in an upper room, is quite as impressive as the larger cabinet which forms the central attraction in the timbered hall of that lovely old Westmorland farm-cottage. Every toy in the Holt Collection has its own individual history; how it was collected, and the circumstances surrounding its "toy-life." This is, of course, common to most collectors' pieces, but the intrinsic elements of folk-art with which many old toys are invested make these relevant anecdotes extremely attractive.

Since it is customary to abrogate such an interest to the domain

[1] Barbara Jones, *Unsophisticated Arts.*

111. Scene from *Robinson Crusoe*, reproduced by colour lithography, to give three-dimensional effect in a mid-nineteenth-century cut-out toybook

112. Group of table tops including Tee-To-Tum and Swedish spinning novelty

113. Some items from the collection of Mme F. Fastré
114. Noah's Ark with marquetry finish, and hand-carved animals, probably French

of youth, why, the question arises, do adults collect toys ? I have found, through discussing their reasons with various collectors, that something quite incidental started them off on a path which, as all collecting does, led to a deepening knowledge and a widening of horizons not to be attained by other means.

Gordon Craig, it will be remembered, favoured the cheap English wooden toys, about which he wrote so feelingly in his little book:

"In fact, in every way the penny wooden toy is as superior to a sixpenny metal one as the wooden Warship 'Victory' is to H.M.S. 'Horrible'—Ironclad. In an old cupboard, behind the little pane of glass they look far more beautiful than most china, and a mass of them make a blaze of colour not to be beaten. It is difficult to get an 'Oilcake Crusher' or an 'Admiral' nowadays."[1]

The artist, then, without exception is attracted by beauty, simplicity and ingenuity in design. When I first met Madame Fia Fastré, the Anglo-Belgian international pianist and folk-parodist, I realised that her motives for collecting also spring from her life as an artist.

It was during her career as a concert pianist, travelling from country to country, that Madame Fastré, instead of accepting the conventional floral tribute from her musical admirers, would suggest, with an inscrutability that often puzzled them, that if they insisted on flattering her with a memento from their town or homeland, what she would delight in most was simply—a toy!

In this way came to be assembled, now all happily housed in her cherished "museum" (which was originally a garage) at Chalfont St. Giles, a unique collection of toys from most countries in the world (113, 116). These are characterised by the virtue of craftsmanship, and are all entirely free from the vulgar or the pointless.

The selection shown in the illustration (113) are all English, and moving from left to right are:

First group (English)
Stile with Dog Toby, made by a disabled soldier, and sold for a penny after 1914-1918 war, in the streets of High Wycombe.
Kim the Pup. Made in Lord Robert's workshop about 1920.
Cottage cut from chalk.
Doulton's copy of twelfth-century jug and mugs.

The second group (116) are indicative of the folk-quality in toys which Madame Fastré has particularly valued. These include the following examples:

[1] *Book of Penny Toys,* Preface.

Second group
   Instrumental whistle. *Jugoslavian.*
   Elephant. *Indian.*
   Egg-shell toys and bird whistle. *Czechoslovakian.*
   Bog-oak jaunting car. *Irish.*

Miss Marjorie Parkes, of Purley, began collecting dolls quite recently. It was on account of her interest in fashion and dress that her hobby took on momentum.

It was through her friend Dr. C. Willet Cunnington, an authority on the history of costume, that she acquired her first Victorian doll. Thus the flame of her interest was fanned. Today, arranged according to nationality on a large table in the one-time Billiard Room, stands in colourful serried ranks, and living in complete harmony, an Assembly of the United Nations of dolls! Local charities and hospitals, and, of course, some privileged fortunate children, benefit from the fact that this remarkable collection is centred in Surrey.

There are many doll collectors in this country and they are now, through their painstaking and patient activities, helping to keep as part of the heritage of Britain some of the very beautiful dolls which might otherwise be taken out of the country.

Miss Nancy Catford, an illustrator of children's books, and a sculptress in wood, had her initial interest logically through the texture of wooden toys. Her work as designer, artist and toy-expert grew from the practical experience which she gained while running a toy factory at Welwyn for several years.

It was through his professional interest in *coiffeur* that Mr. Steiner, who collects musical automata, first started his hobby. Spying out an old doll with an interesting hair style in a store at Bruges, he bought her and took her home with thoughts of dressing her hair—perhaps for a window display. When he began to undress the doll he found inside a hard contrivance which soon convinced him that she had been a clockwork musical figure.

From that day his interest was aroused; his unique collection of mechanical musical dolls is growing from year to year. In repairing some of these he made interesting discoveries—for example, that an old newspaper, used in the interior of his Monkey Harpist, dated it at 1800. Yet the tune played by the box is by Offenbach, who was not born until 1819. The incompatibility is explained by the probability of a new movement having been fitted after the doll had been made, at a time when Offenbach's popularity was at its height.

Very few people have made a hobby of collecting musical boxes, musical watches, organettes and singing birds. This select company includes Mr. E. R. Pole of Wiltshire, whose comprehensive collection of musical movements, representative of Swiss and French craftsmen, was exhibited at the Science Museum at Kensington during the early part of 1949, where it aroused much attention.

Another important collection is owned by Mr. Percy Muir, the bibliophile and publisher. He first became interested in toys through a love of the theatre. In his early days he was a music-hall artiste, and began by collecting toy theatres. From then, little by little, his interest in books and the arts deepened. He acquired strange and rare mechanical toys, automata, table games and board games, until his present home at Takeley is, for all the world, like a chapter from a romantic story-book in the mind of a child. His acquisitions from the famous Bussell Toy Collection have added to its historical value, while the number of Victorian educational toys, book-toys, ephemeral panoramas and jigsaws amassed by the original owner lend to it an antiquarian significance rare among toy collections. Students of toy history will always feel indebted to connoisseurs like Percy Muir, whose admiration for, and appreciation of, originality in toy-making have helped to preserve in this country for posterity unique examples which might otherwise have been lost entirely.

When I met Mrs. Alison Uttley at her lovely woodland cottage in Buckinghamshire it was like entering a world full of warmth, innocence and old-world charm. What else might one expect from the author of *Country Things* and the *Little Grey Rabbit* books? Here I was shown the very toys which Alison Uttley played with when a child and mentioned in her own writings. They must now be familiar to many people through those studies of a Victorian childhood.

Miss Barbara Jones, a student of Victoriana, was the organiser in the summer of 1951 of an unusual exhibition put on at the Whitechapel Art Gallery, entitled "Black Eyes and Champagne."

It was an attempt to make the public conscious of those very ordinary and everyday things which have played a significant role in English life, with special emphasis laid on unsophisticated basic design and the materials used.

Several historical toys were loaned, including dolls' houses, rocking-horses and a large selection of metal and lead wheel-toys of the mid-nineteenth century.

As a result of the exhibition, Miss Jones herself became interested in Lord Mayor's coaches. The illustration is from her collection and shows three different contemporary designs, one being gilded, the others in tarnished, unpainted lead (115).

The second group contains wooden toys from Ceylon, two horses brightly decorated and varnished, and an assembly of citizens, five men and a woman (118). They are in an excellent state of repair. Many of these toys from India and Ceylon were brought back to England by planters and members of the Forces returning on leave. It is for this reason that they are preserved as ornaments in homes where, together with mother-of-pearl lacquered trays from Japan and balancing-toys from China, they are treasured more as heirlooms, and are no longer regarded as children's playthings.

Of all the categories favoured by adult collectors, the costume doll is the most widespread, and enjoys an ever-growing circle of devotees. This form of collecting began as a fashion among women, who would acquire expensively dressed mascot-dolls to use as ornaments in their rooms, either placed on a settee or propped up on a dressing-table. The interest was extended when many European countries began to offer costume dolls in national dress as mementoes. Publicised by the tourist trade, these took the form of presents calculated to spread international goodwill and understanding.

The craze reached its height between the wars, when some countries began to manufacture costume dolls patterned on the national costumes of others—an ambition not without its incongruous and ridiculous aspect.

The collecting of these costume dolls became a vogue among Americans, and in the 1920's added yet another class of item to what may be described as a national propensity for doll-collecting.[1]

In England the making of costume dolls in the form of national types, or as tea-cosies, reflected a love of patient needlecraft which is still a feature of the communal work lovingly undertaken by women who make articles for charities, sales-of-work of annual church bazaars.

The designing of character dolls is a highly specialised art and very few women in England have devoted their leisure entirely to this enthralling hobby. Among them is Mrs. Widdows of Birkdale, Lancashire, whose remarkable collection of costume and character dolls is regularly put on view in different parts of the country exclusively as a means of raising funds in aid of the National Society

[1] Lesley Gordon, *A Pageant of Dolls.*

115. Coaches of the Lord Mayors of London (Barbara Jones Collection)

116. Traditional toys from Mme. F. Fastré's collection
117. Traditional Russian hand-carved farmer and animals, movement induced by scissor-type action

for the Prevention of Cruelty to Children. Visitors to these seasonal exhibitions have commented on the care and accuracy with which the assortment has been executed. Presented in groups, they altogether number one hundred different characters. They are classified to demonstrate differences in national costume, the period dress of famous historical characters, popular creations from the great writers and traditional personalities from juvenile folklore and nursery literature.

It has been seen how the collecting of toys, like the amassing of other curios, has sprung from a variety of motives—artistic, professional, altruistic, or from just an irrational appetite, a form of curiosity quite accidentally satisfied in its incipient phase.

There is, however, a peculiar attraction which toys exercise on grown-ups. This combines a conscious antiquarian appreciation with an unconscious respect for the innate history of a thing which embodies, in a mysterious way, the unexpressed idea that it once may have had a deeply religious function and significance.

Collecting toys is by no means a recent fashion. Gröber has suggested that the habit began towards the end of the Middle Ages when craftsmen who had formerly earned their living making objects for use in churches falling upon lean times, had to turn their hands to making smaller things for private patrons. The demand was for oddities and quaint examples of craftsmanship, and so there arose in the homes of merchants and the nobility the custom of having cabinets made to hold these curios. "Not only at courts or among the wealthy nobility, for the middle-class merchant did not want to be behind in the fashion, and so he started to collect. The new craze stimulated the toy industry, since the loving purpose of giving toys to their little ones seemed to justify the parents in getting such toys made as also appeal, and have ever appealed, to grown-ups."[1]

The toy-maker's aim, apparently, was as much to please the sponsor as his child, and the chances are that the majority of these works of art found their way into the newly commissioned cabinet rather than into the children's rooms of the big houses.

[1] Karl Gröber, *Children's Toys of Bygone Days*, p. 14.

18. Indian and Cingalese traditional figurines in painted and lacquered wood

SOME BRITISH PUBLIC COLLECTIONS

IN LONDON

Bethnal Green Museum
Borough of Dartford Museum
British Museum
Commonwealth Institute
Elder Collection of Dolls, Hammersmith
Geffrye Museum, Shoreditch
Gunnersbury Museum, Middlesex

Horniman Museum, Dulwich
London Museum, Kensington Palace
Pinto Collection, Northwood, Middlesex
Pollock's Toy Museum
Royal United Service Museum
Wellcome Museum, Wellcome Institute
Victoria & Albert Museum

OUTSIDE LONDON

Abbey House Museum, Leeds
Ashmolean Museum, Oxford
Barnard Castle, County Durham
Blithfield Hall, Staffs.
Bristol Folk Museum, Blaise Castle House
Cambridge & County Folk Museum
Castle Museum, Colchester
Chelmsford & Essex Museum
Chester Museum
City Museum, Leeds
Cliff Castle, Keighley
Derby Museum
Doll Museum, Warwick
Dumfries Burgh Museum, Scotland
Fitzwilliam Museum, Cambridge
Folk Museum Cambridge
Harris Museum, Preston
Helston Museum, Cornwall (a few)
Hereford City Museum
Hollytrees Museum, Colchester
Hove Museum, Sussex
Kirkstall Abbey, Leeds
Lanhydrock House, Bodmin, Cornwall
Longford Castle, Near Salisbury
Luton Museum, Bedfordshire

Museum of Childhood, Edinburgh
National Museum of Wales
Peterborough Museum, Northants
Pitt Rivers Museum, Oxford
Pitt Rivers Museum, Farnham Royal, Dorset
Priest's House, West Hoathly
Queen's Park Art Gallery, Manchester
Red House, Christchurch, Hants.
Royal Scottish Museum, Edinburgh
Salisbury Museum, Wiltshire
St. Albans Museum, Hertfordshire
Saltwell Park Museum, Gateshead
Shibden Hall, Halifax
Snowshill Manor, Gloucestershire
Somerset County Museum, Taunton
Tollcross Museum, Glasgow
Toy Museum, Rottingdean, Brighton
Truro Museum, Cornwall (a few)
Tunbridge Wells Museum
Warwick Doll Museum
Windsor Castle, Windsor
Woburn Abbey, Bedfordshire
Worthing Museum, Sussex
York Castle Museum

BIBLIOGRAPHY

Abercromby, John. *The Pre- and Proto-historic Times.*
d'Allemagne, Henri René. *Histoire des Jouets*, Paris, 1903. *Les Jouets à la World's Fair en* 1904 *à Saint Louis*, Paris, 1908. *La très véridique histoire de Nette et Tintin visitant le village du jouet*, Paris, 1927.
Anderson, Madge. *Heroes of the Puppet Stage*, Jonathan Cape, London.
Bakushinsky, A. *Clay Toys of Vyatka Province*, Russia, 1929.
Bailey, C. S. *Tops and Whistles*, Viking, New York, 1937.
Baldet, Marcel. *Figurines et Soldats de Plomb.* Paris.
Bartram, N. D. *The Toy—Joy of Children*, 1912. *Concerning New Trends*, 1930.
Becque de Fouquières, L. *Les jeux des anciens*, Paris, 1869.
Bek de Fuker. *Games of the Ancients*, 1877.
Benua, A. *The Russian National Toy*, 1905.
Best, Ebsdon. *Games and Pastimes of the Maori*, Wellington, 1925.
Bestelmeier, Georg Hieronymus. *Magazin von verschiedener Kunst*, 1803, 1807.
Bettex, A. (Editor). *Du*, Toy Supplement, Zürich, November 1951.
Bobrinsky, A. A. *Volkstümliche russische Holzarbeiten*, Moscow, 1910.
Boesch, Hans. *Kinderleben in der deutschen Vergangenheit*, Leipzig, 1900.
Bogdanov, B. B. *On the Study of Toys*, 1912.
Böhn, M. von. *Puppen*, etc., 2 vols, 1929. Trans. 1932.
Booth, H. *Playthings*, Bureau of Educational Experiments, New York, 1917.
Boruck, V. N. *The Peasant Toy Industry of Moscow Province*, 1912.
Böttiger, John. *Philipp Hainhofer und der Kunstschrank Gustav Adolfs in Upsala*, Stockholm, 1909-10.
Broek, Otta van Tussen. *De Toegepaste Kunsten in Nederland*, Rotterdam, 1925.
Brubaker, Miriam. *A Century of Progress in Toys*, Washington, 1944.
Bryant, G. E. *Chelsea Porcelain Toys*, 1745-84, London, 1925.
Bück, Joseph. *Das Puppentheater*, in "Zeitschrift für die Interessen aller Puppenspieler und für Geschichte und Technik aller Puppentheater," Leipzig, 1923 ff.
Caiger, G. *Dolls on Display—Japan in Miniature*, Japan, 1933.
Calmettes, Pierre. *Les Joujoux*, Paris, 1924.
Campbell, M. W. *Paper Toy Making*, Pitman, London, 1937.
Canning, Wright. *Peeps at the World's Dolls*, New York, 1953.
Cata, J. M. *International Trade in Toys*, U.S. Bureau of Commerce, Trade Information Bulletin 445.
Catford, Nancy. *Making Nursery Toys*, London, 1944.
Cavestony, Julio. *El Arte Industrial de los Juguetes Esporales*, Spain, 1944.
Ceretilli. *Russian Peasant Toys*, Moscow, 1933.
Chamberlaine, B. H. *Things Japanese*, 1880.
Chapuis, André. *Les Automates*, Geneva, 1952.
Charizina, V. *Toys of Primitive Peoples*, 1912.

Chushkin, A. *Toys Carved from Wood*, 1927.

Claretie, Leo. *Les Jouets, histoire, fabrication*, Paris, 1894. *Une Collection des Poupées en Costumes Populaires*, Paris, 1901.

Clark, V. S. *History of Toy Manufacture in the United States (1860-1893)*.

Cooke, Conrad William. *Automata Old and New*, Chiswick Press, London.

Craig, Gordon. *The Mask* (periodical), Florence, 1915. *The Marionette Tonight at 12.30*, Florence, 1918.

Daiken, L. H. *Children's Games Throughout the Year*, London, 1949. *Teaching Through Play*, Pitman, 1953.

Delachaux, Théodor. *Jouets rustiques Suisses*, in the "Schweizerisches Archiv für Volkskunde," 1914.

Denshina, A. *Dressed Dolls of Russia*, 1919.

Dinces, G. A. *The Russian Clay Toy*, 1936.

Donderkery, K. *Journey through Toyland*, Bombay, 1954.

Dunton, J. *A Compleat History of the Most Remarkable Providences that have happened in this Present Age*, London, 1697.

Early, Alice K. *English Effigies, Dolls and Puppets*, London, 1955.

Early, Mabel. *Toy Making*, London, 1944.

Eatright, J. F., and Young, B. M. *Adventuring with Toy Activities*, Bureau of Public Teaching Colleges, Colombia University, New York.

Edelman, C. E. *The Making of Soft Toys*, London, 1931.

Eder, M. *Spillgrate* (Folklore Studies VI). *Summaries in English*, Peiping, 1947.

Erle, T. W. *Science in the Nursery or Children's Toys and What They Teach*, London, 1884.

Evdokimov, I. *The Russian Toy*, 1925.

Exner, William. *Die Hausindustrie Oesterreichs*, Vienna, 1890.

Feldhaus, Franz, M. *Die Technik*, 1914.

Forrer, Robert. *Les Etains de la Collection Alfred Ritleng*, Strassburg, 1903.

Fournier, Edouard. *Histoire des Jouets et des jeux d'enfants*, Paris, 1889.

Freeman, Ruth and Larry. *Cavalcade of Toys*, New York, 1942. *The Child and His Picture Book*, Chicago, 1933.

Galkin, I. *Toys from Paper*, Russia, 1926.

Games and Toys Year Book for 1951, London.

Gandini, L. A. *Di una puppattola*, d. sec. 15, 1886.

Garratt, John G. *Model Soldiers*.

Gatterer, Christoph, W. J. *Technologisches Magazin*, Memmingen, 1790–92.

Geist, F., and Mahlau, A. *Spielzeug*, Leipzig, 1938.

Gennert, A. *Toys from Cloth*, Russia, 1926.

Glagol, S. *Russian Folk Toys of the Nineteenth Century*, 1912.

Gordon, Lesley. *A Pageant of Dolls*, Edmund Ward, London.

Grant, J. *The Doll's House*, Studio, London, 1934.

Grasberger, Lorenz. *Erziehung und Unterricht im Klassischen Altertum*, Würzburg, 1864.

Gray, A. J. *Post-War Condition of the German Toy Industry*, U.S. Foreign Trade Bulletin, 267, 1924.

Gremer. *Children's Toys*, London, 1873.

Greene, Vivien. *English Dolls' Houses*, 1955.

Gregor and von Sydow. *Leishens Puppenstube*, Berlin, 1884.

Gröber, Karl. *Children's Toys of Bygone Days*, Batsford, London, 1928.

Gross, August. *Ritterliches Spielzeug*, in the "Festschrift für Julius Schlosser," Vienna, 1926.

Gumuchian et cie. *Les Livres de l'enfance du XVe au XIXe siècle*, Paris, 1930.

Haberlandt, A. *Die Holzschnitzerei im Grödener Tale*, in the "Werke der Volkskunst," Vienna, 1914.

Hallwylska, S. *Beskrifvande förteckning*, Stockholm, 1934.

Hampe, Theodor. *Der Zinnsoldat. Ein deutsches Spielzeug*, Berlin, 1924.

Harris, Henry. *Model Soldiers*, 1962.

Harrison, E. *Christmastide, and the Place of Toys in the Education of the Child*, Chicago, 1902.

Hartmann, August. *Zur Geschichte der Berchtesgadener Schnitzerei*, in "Volkskunst und Volkskunde," Munich, 1903.

Heatherington, M. G., and Underhill, M. C. *Simple Toy Making for Pleasure and Profit*, Pearson, London, 1925.

Herčík, Emanuel. *Folktoys of Czechoslovakia*, 1952, Prague.

Hertz, Louis H. *The Handbook of Old American Toys*, Mark Haber, 1947.

Hincs, Hilda. *Modern Soft Toys and How to Make Them*, London, 1938.

Hirn, Yriö. *Les jeux d'enfants*, Paris, 1926.

Hobrecker, Karl. *Alte vergessene Kinderbücher*, Berlin, 1924.

Hoffmann-Drayer, E. *Heimberger Keramik*, in the "Schweizerisches Archiv für Volkskunde," 1914.

Holme, C. G. *Children's Toys of Yesterday*, Special Winter Supplement of "The Studio," 1932.

Hooper, Elizabeth. *American Historical Dolls*, 1952.

Horth, A. C. *I Made it Myself*, Batsford, London, 1941.

Huizinga, J. *Homo Ludens—A Study of the Play Element in Culture*, London, 1949.

Institut Pédagogique National, *Jeux et Jouets*, Paris, 1962.

Jackson, E. Nevill. *Toys of Other Days*, London, 1907.

Jacobs, Flora Gill. *A History of Dolls' Houses.*

Johl, J. P. *The Fascinating Story of Dolls*, Lindquist, New York, 1941. *More About Dolls*, 1946. *Your Dolls and Mine*, 1952.

Jones, Barbara. *The Unsophisticated Arts*, London, 1951.

Jouets, Les, et Jeux Anciens. "Bulletin illustré de la Société des Amateurs des Jouets et Jeux Anciens," 1905 ff.

Journal des Luxus und der Moden, Vol. VII, Weimar, 1791.

Kawin, E. *The Wise Choice of Toys*, Chicago, 1938.

Kay, J., and C. T. White, *Toys, Their Design and Construction*, 1944.

Lambert, M., and Marx, E. *English Popular Art*, Batsford, London, 1951.

Ledesma, G. Fernandez. *Juguetes Mexicanos*, Mexico, 1930.

Lessing, Julius, and Brüning, Adolf. *Der Pommersche Kunstschrank*, Berlin, 1905.

Lewis, Mary E. *The Marriage of Diamonds and Dolls.*

Lézan, Claude. *Les Poupées Anciennes*, Paris, 1930.

Liefmann, Robert. *Über Wesen und Formen des Verlags*, Freiburg, 1899.

Lill, Georg. *Nürnberger Zinnfiguren der Familie Hilpert*, in "Kunst und Handwerk," Munich, 1920.

Lovett. *The Child's Doll: Origin, Legend, Folklore*, 1915.

Low, Frances H. *Oueen Victoria's Dolls,* Newnes, 1894.

Macy's Book of Sports and Pastimes, R. H. Macy, New York, 1885.

Magnin, Charles. *Histoire des Marionettes en Europe,* Paris, 1852.

Makinson, J. T. *Toy Manufacture,* Funk & Wagnalls, New York, 1931.

Martin, P. and Vaillant, M. *Le Monde Merveilleux des Soldats de Plomb.*

McLeish, M., and Horton, Winifred M. *Wooden Toy Making,* 1936.

Meyer, Gertrud. *Die Spielwarenindustrie im säschsischen Erzgebirge,* Leipzig, 1911.

Mochrie, E., and Roseamon, I. P. *Felt Toys,* 1931.

Moody, Edith. *Dressed Soft Toys,* 1937.

Moroder, Franz. *Das Grödner Thal,* St. Ulrich in Gröden, 1891.

Mosoriak, Roy. *The Curious History of Music Boxes,* Lightner Publishing Company, Chicago.

Muller, S., and Professor Vogelsang. *Holländische Patrizierhäuser,* Utrecht, 1907.

Oman, C. *English Silver Toys,* in "Apollo Miscellany," 1950.

Pearce, Cyril. *Toys and Models,* Batsford, London, 1948.

Pick, J. B. *Dictionary of Games,* London, 1953.

Provence, Marcel. *Nouvelle Histoire du Sariton.*

Rausch, Ernst. *Die Sonneberger Spielwaren-Industrie,* Berlin, 1901.

Richter, W. *Die Spiele der Griechen und Römer,* Leipzig, 1887.

Rogers, Dorothy. *Paper Dolls: French Provincial Costumes.*

Rosenhaupt, Karl. *Die Nürnberger-Fürther Metallwarenindustrie in geschichtlicher und sozial-politischer Beleuchtung,* Stuttgart and Berlin, 1907.

Roth, Johann F. *Geschichte des Nürnbergischen Handels,* 1800.

St. George, Eleanor. *The Dolls of Yesterday; Dolls of Three Centuries,* Scribner, 1951.

Sansea, L. *La Bimeloterie,* Paris, 1917. *Le Jouet,* Paris, 1917.

Saunders, Francis. *Puppetry in Schools.*

Sax, Emanuel. *Die Hausindustrie in Thüringen,* Jena, 1885.

Schlosser, Julius von. *Die Kunst- und Wunderkammern der Spätrenaissance,* Leipzig, 1908.

Schmidt, Eva Altschlesien. *Mittelalterliche Spielzeugpferdchen und Toureiter,* 1934.

Schmoller, Gustav. *Zur Geschichte der deutschen Kleingewerbe im 19. Jahrhundert,* Halle, 1870.

Schultz, Alwin. *Das höfische Leben zur Zeit der Minnesinger,* Leipzig, 1889. *Das häusliche Leben der europäischen Kulturvölker vom Mittelalter bis zur zweiten Hälfte des XVIII Jahrhunderts,* Munich and Berlin, 1903.

Senst, Otto. *Die Metallspielwarenindustrie und der Spielwarenhandel von Nürnberg und Fürth,* Erlangen, 1901.

Seyfert, Otto, and Trier, W. *Spielzeug,* Berlin, 1923.

Shinkokai, Kokusai Bunka. *Poupées Japonaises,* Tokio.

Sinclair, H. *Toy Manufacture and Marketing,* Springfield, Philips, 1931.

Singleton, E. *Dolls,* 1927.

Sloane, G. *Electric Toy Making for Amateurs.*

Soviet Toys, An Interdepartmental Bulletin on Toys including contributions from the State Museums, 1931.

Speaight, George. *Juvenile Drama—The History of the Toy Theatre,* London, 1946.

Starr, F. *Japanese Toys,* 3 vols, 1926.

Stowe, Wilbur Macy. *Paper Dolls and other Cut-out Toys,* Newark Museum.

Strutt, J. *Sports and Pastimes of the British People.*

Taylor, E. S. *History of Playing Cards.*

Tippett, J. S. *Toys and Toy Makers,* Harper Brothers, New York, 1931.

Toy Manufacturing Association, *Toy Manufacturers in the U.S.A.,* New York, 1935.

Trier, W., and Seyfert, O. *Toys,* 1923.

Tseretelli, N. *Russkaya Krestyanskaya Igruski (The Russian Peasant Toy),* "Academia," 1933.

Valeri, Malaguzzi F. *Arte gaia,* 1926.

Vanalstyne, D. *Play Behaviour and Children's Play Materials,* University of Chicago Press, 1932.

Vaux, F. B. (Vulpius). *Domestic Pleasures. Curiositäten der physisch-literarisch-artistisch-historischen Vor- und Mitwelt zur angenehmen Unterhaltung für gebildete Leser,* Weimar, 1812 ff.

Weatherley, T. E. *Punch and Judy.*

Weigel, Christoff. *Abbildung der gemeinnützlichen Haupt-Stande von denen Regenten bis auf alle Künstler und Handwerker,* Regensburg, 1698.

Weismantel, Leo. *Werkbuch der Puppenspiele,* Berlin, 1924. *Die Bücherei der Puppenspiele,* Berlin, 1925.

Wenham Historical Library. *Files of Antiques and Playthings.*

Westenberger, Bernhard. *Die Holzspielwarenindustrie im sächsischen Erzgebirge,* Leipzig, 1911.

Westermanns. *Von Spiel und Spielzeug,* Düsseldorf, 1906.

White, Gwen. *A Book of Toys,* Penguin Books, London. *A Picture Book of Ancient and Modern Toys. Dolls of the World,* 1963.

Whitehouse, F. R. B. *Table Games,* London, 1951.

Wilson, A. E. *Penny Plain, Twopence Coloured,* Macmillan, London, 1932.

Yameda, Tokubei, *Japanese Dolls,* Tokyo, 1955.

Zinnfigur, Die. *Bundesblatt des deutschen Zinnfigures-sammlerbundes "Clio,"* Berlin, 1927.

Zinnsoldat, Der standhafte. *Monatsschrift für Zinnfigurensammler,* Hannover, 1924 ff.

INDEX

The numerals in **heavy type** denote the figure numbers of the illustrations.